ONE STEP

to

WEALTH

Published in 1999 by 23rd St. Press
15165 Yonge Street, Suite 201
Aurora, Ontario L4G IMI

Toll Free: 1 (888) 367•7450
Phone: (905) 713•3765
Fax: (905) 713•2937
E-mail: mail@bellfinancial.on.ca
Website: www.bellfinancial.on.ca

CANADIAN CATALOGUING IN PUBLICATION DATA

Bell, William, 1957-
    One step to wealth

    ISBN 0-9686415-0-4

    1. Finance, Personal. 2. Retirement income—Planning. I. Title.
HG179.B446 2000   332.024'01   C00-910026-1

CREDITS:
Project Manager & Editor: Janet Alford / RedStone, Calgary, Alberta
Interior Design & Production Management: Jeremy Drought / Last Impression Publishing Service, Calgary, Alberta
Proof Reader: Wayne Magnuson / Prairie House Books, Calgary, Alberta
Cover Design: The Cat's Meow Design Inc., Calgary, Alberta
Back Cover Photo of Author: Richard Allan, Photographer, Aurora, Ontario

Printed and bound in Canada by Friesens, Altona, Manitoba

ONE STEP

to

WEALTH

*. . . you're **that** close*

to the life you want

WILLIAM BELL

23rd **ST.**
PRESS

DEDICATION

In loving memory of my father

W. Henry Bell

Acknowledgements

THIS is surprisingly difficult to write, not because I find it hard to say thanks, but rather because I don't know where to draw the line with respect to whom to thank. It's easy to argue that everyone who has touched my life since birth has had an influence on what you will read here. Can I name them all? I guess not.

Here then is my short list of people who have most directly been a part of this project. Warmest thanks to:

My wife and partner in everything, **Ellen**—for believing, and helping me to believe. Love *is* the greatest inspiration. My daughters, **Leah, Deandra**, and **Alexis**, for joyously teaching me every day about life, love and priorities. My mom, **Phyllis Bell**, and my father, the late **Henry Bell**, whose enduring gifts I have only begun to realize and understand in the context of raising my own children.

My associates and staff—**David Frank, Tad Gacich, Tracey Hough, Rob Kimball, Nona Morrow, Laurie Sobie, Sonia Thomas**, and **Tan Yen Yap**—for allowing me to pursue a dream. **Ted** and **Susan Chant**—for their incredible support and friendship. **Janet Alford**—for her wonderful work as editor and project manager, and for her kindness, compassion, and commitment to this book. **Ross Gilchrist**—for sharing his many talents. He has an uncanny ability to show up at key points in my life and make a huge difference. This is one such time. **Arlen Keyes**—for giving me confidence and support, and helping me move from an idea to a real project. **David Barker**—for encouragement, his time and his expertise. **Glen Reid**—for being my "Jedi master," my mentor, and my friend, and thus helping me find the courage to begin. **Jeremy Drought**—for his excellent work and sincere, heart-felt interest in this project's success.

And to **Vince Savoia**, **Brad Davis**, **Stu Field**, Graham **Cochrane**, a whole bunch of other people at *Manulife Financial*, **Catina Despotopoulos**, **Neal Kearney**, **Andrew Weening**, and countless friends and clients who have encouraged, and inspired.

To all of those named here, and to all others who have contributed, even in a small way, I say "thanks." My gratitude will find its way to you in ways we can't imagine. Such is the power of giving.

CONTENTS

INTRODUCTION

I grew up in a small town, in a family of average means. For most of my childhood, however, I believed we were rich. Not rich in the sense of flying around in private jets, but rich in the truest sense of all. I believed that if I wanted something, and it was good, I could have it—and moreover, I would get it. I honestly can't recall a single situation in my childhood where that didn't hold true.

One of the more unfortunate aspects of growing up is the realization that money *doesn't* grow on trees. With respect to money, growing up really boils down to learning how to worry. Ironically, it doesn't matter how much we have, we still instinctively worry. We worry mostly of course about not having enough. Then we worry about losing what we have—or more accurately, losing *any* of what we have. We worry that we aren't keeping up with more aggressive investors, or that we are taking too *much* risk. Most of all, we worry that because we don't know enough about money, we are probably making lots of big mistakes. The truth of the matter is, the *only* mistake we really make is in worrying at all.

The more I learn, and probably the older and wiser I get, the more I realize that I had it right when I was a kid. I *can* have anything I want. I don't need to worry about money (or anything else for that matter). And most important of all, I *am* rich.

OK, that's me, and this book isn't about me. It's about you. And if you are reading this book, chances are you wish you had more money, and quite frankly, you don't care about how much I have, or think I have. Rightly so. You're reading this book hoping that it will contain the "magic recipe" for financial success.

Well, I believe that it does.

It will interest you to know that this "recipe" is written in countless other books, many of which you have probably read. So I am telling you what you have already heard. But, it's quite likely you need to, and want to, hear it again. It's a message that is too simple, and too easy, to be readily believed.

I have purposely tried to keep this book simple and to the point. Not because I underestimate the reader's intelligence—but rather because our intelligence actually gets in the way. This isn't something to be intellectualized. It is a message that needs to become a part of the way you see yourself and the world.

It all boils down to a few simple things that we almost universally believe to be true, and yet they are not true. We need to convince ourselves to stop believing in lies, and the truth will emerge.

Read on, and discover for yourself how easy it is.

1

Getting Rich in
Three Two One Steps

*"All great truths are simple in the final analysis, and easily understood;
if they are not, they are not great truths."*
Napoleon Hill

WE live in a paradoxical world.

For example, on one hand, we want "the good life." A life of balance and purpose. A life of fulfillment. A life of calm, peace and happiness. A life of meaning. A life without worry.

On the other hand, we have an ongoing obsession with a success formula that looks much different. We work too much. We lack fulfillment. Our life is hurried, scattered, and unfocused. We search for a shred of meaning. And most of all, we worry.

The troubling thing is that we tolerate these unhappy realities; in fact, we welcome them, because we believe they are the ticket to the good life. Most of us apparently believe that the road to paradise travels first through purgatory.

> *"Many receive advice,
> only the wise profit from it."*
> Syrus

At the center of this paradoxical struggle, is money.

Only money will solve our problems. We can do the things we really want to do—when we have enough money. We can relax—

when we have enough money. We will find true meaning—when we have enough money. We can stop worrying—when we have enough money.

"The good life," it would seem for most of us, is a life with lots of money.

This isn't a book that will try to convince you that you should be happy with what you have, or worse, with less than you want. I won't be trying to convince you that money is the evil source of your problems. But neither will I try to convince you that money is the *answer* to all of your problems.

This is a book about helping you get what you want, and what you want can be quite literally anything. Since many "things" in life are bought with money, and since money is undeniably something we believe will help us find peace and happiness in our lives, we will focus our attention on the attainment of wealth.

But an even more important reason to use money as our target of attainment is that for most of us, it is the greatest obstacle in our path. Conquering the power that money has over our lives and turning that into a power we can have over money will open literally thousands of doors that previously were locked.

This is a "how to" book. At times it won't appear that it is. That's because we are conditioned to believe that how-to books lead us through a series of physical steps. In fact, we are quite obsessed with discovering and applying physical steps to a vast array of important goals. Five Steps to Better Health, Ten Steps to a Better Marriage, The Eight-Step Weight-Loss Program...that sort of thing. This book *is* a step-by-step guide, except there's really only one step.

This idea—that there is only one step—will likely cause skepticism. Furthermore, you might wonder why articulating one step takes a book of this size. Let me explain.

The reason that so many of the multi-step programs don't work is that we tend to skip over the steps we don't like. We focus instead on the one or two steps that we like the best, either hopeful, or actually believing, that this short-cut approach will work for us. We eat right, but don't exercise, or we communicate openly with our spouse, but only when we have the time, and we cut down on our fat intake, but hey, we aren't giving up anything we really *like*.

When it comes to financial success (and arguably success in anything) there is one step that is almost universally accepted as important. This one important step is quite frequently skipped over. In fact, when it comes specifically to accumulating wealth, or retirement planning, we almost *always* skip over it, or at the very least, cover it quickly. And our lack of attention to this one step ultimately causes our failure. Conversely, attention to this one step all but guarantees our success.

Consider the simple steps to achievement and you will see what I mean. The three steps to financial success, actually the three steps to success in *anything*, are these:

1. Decide exactly what you want.
2. Plan to get it.
3. Put the plan in motion.

Now, look these steps over. You may be thinking that this is too trivial. You may wonder if you have wasted your money buying this book. You may already be trying to pencil in the steps that you know are missing. But hang on. Think about this. This is how you go about doing *everything*. Most of the things we do are so routine to us we don't realize we are actually going through this process. But even as you read this, your brain has already decided that at the end of the page it will give your muscles the instructions to turn the page over. You know what you want, the plan is formulated, and the plan is in motion!

Anyhow, we can debate the merits of this particular set of success steps and perhaps the specific wording of each step, but that would be veering off course. The purpose of this dialogue is to point out that there is one, and only one, *indispensable* step on the road to wealth. And looking at these steps, or even a longer or different list that you may wish to substitute, it's pretty obvious which step is *indispensable*. Before you can plan to get something (or be something), you have to know what it is. Simple to the point of absurdity.

But here's the really absurd thing. Most people have not taken this all-important step with respect to their financial lives. Many people have a plan in place—they've moved on to steps two and three, but step number one remains a mystery. Virtually all of us "plan" to get more money, or spend less, or pay less tax, or "get rich," but we have no idea what the real target—the real goal—looks like. It's like building a house with no plan and no picture of the finished product.

At this stage it's common to start rationalizing as to why you *haven't* set specific financial goals, or to convince yourself that in fact *you have*. Don't do that, just yet at least…we'll look at this process later. Let's first think more deeply about this three-step, or arguably one-step, process.

Think of the last thing you did that required significant thought or planning. It might have been purchasing a new car, or a new home, or taking a vacation. At some point you *decided* that you would. Once you decided, you set out to plan how. If it was buying a car, for example, you went for some test drives and started negotiating with the sellers. At this point, of course, it's all over.

Once you made the *decision* to buy the new car, it was as good as in the driveway.

Let's make a distinction between deciding and wishing. When we wish for something we don't believe we can have it. If you simply wish you could have a new car it's not a good idea to go out looking for one as this only serves to make you more unhappy about the fact that you can't have what you want. If you go out looking for a new car, expecting to buy one, you have made a decision. It's important to understand the importance of belief here, as *disbelief* is the number one reason for deciding *not* to pursue something we want. We'll deal with belief in more detail later on.

Consider another example—taking a vacation. You have booked the time off from work. You've discussed the vacation with your family or those accompanying you (if anyone) and *made the decision* to go somewhere. It's all but done. Sure you maybe haven't decided where, and how much you'll spend, and how you'll get there. But those are the details, and they *won't* stand in the way of your taking a vacation. It's a big world. You'll find somewhere to go that suits your budget and tastes.

The point here is this. Once you have *decided* on a specific end result, the rest is academic. It just unfolds like a road map.

This appears logical in the case of buying a house, or a car, or taking a vacation. But what if your goal is to become wealthy? (I'll try to stick to the theme.) It seems a little simplistic to suggest that all we have to do is *decide* to become wealthy and voila, the rest will just "happen," and indeed it is.

We know what a car looks like, and we can quickly narrow our search for a new car to those that appeal to us. We know what a vacation is, and within the parameters of our budget and our recreational interests we can find a vacation that satisfies our desires.

But what does it mean to be wealthy? In truth, most of us don't know. You see the problem here is that "wealthy" is not a specific goal. We can't develop a plan to get to Shangri-La because it's not on any map. But we *can* plan a trip to Paris.

> "*This one step—choosing a goal and sticking to it—changes everything.*"
> SCOTT REED

What we need is a *specific* destination. Then we can plan a course of action to reach that destination. Then we can start getting emotionally involved with the end result. Soon we will start to believe that our goal will be realized. And it will.

I know. This just seems to be *too* simple. Go back to the start of this chapter and reread the quote by Napoleon Hill. Then return and carry on. We'll wait.

Pick up literally *any* book on financial planning, especially retirement planning, and you will find this step at the beginning of the book. You will read that you need to set goals. It most likely will be covered in a matter of a few pages, and then virtually never mentioned again. The industry that promotes your financial well-being apparently considers this to be less important than is claimed here. There are many reasons for that, which are covered in detail in this book.

But here are some sobering thoughts.

Financial independence—or more bluntly, having a lot more money—is pretty much a universal desire. Information on this subject is without limit, and access is increasing. Libraries and bookstores have countless titles on how to get and keep more money. Financial planners, investment advisors, and financial gurus abound, and these people are offering seminars virtually every night of the week.

Yet we remain a nation who puts money worries at the very top of the list of things we worry about, and the list of things we find most difficult to talk about. We aren't wealthy. We are heavily in debt. We worry about having enough money to retire. Heck, we worry about having enough money to pay the bills next month.

Currently, barely 2% of Canadians who reach retirement age are able to support themselves without the assistance of Government benefits. The baby boomers, who are in position to wreak havoc on the social support system, seem no better prepared.

> *"Those who cannot tell what they desire or expect still sigh and struggle with indefinite thoughts and vast wishes."*
> RALPH WALDO EMERSON

What's wrong?

Here's what's wrong. We are running around like a bunch of lemmings, trying to find the golden land, but we have no idea what it looks like or where it is. Frankly, we could be sitting in the middle of it and not recognize it. We have a map in the glove compartment, but we won't use it. We don't know how to use it, and it scares us. It scares us, because we'd have to admit we don't have a particular destination. Maps are only useful if you know where you want to go.

The problem is, in one sentence—*we don't know what we want.*

Oh, we *all* know we want money, and lots of it, yet only a few—precious few, in fact—have it. That's because only a few—precious few—have actually made specific goals to acquire it.

OK you may be saying, yea yea, I *have* a financial goal.

Let's see.

Grab a pen or pencil. Now in the space overleaf, write the exact age you plan to retire or at least be financially able to retire. Next, write the exact dollar amount you will need to have in your investments in order to be able to do that.

Age of retirement: Age _____

Total investment balance needed: $ _____

If you are like most Canadians, you were able to fill in the age of retirement (and you likely chose one of 55, 60 or 65) but the total dollar amount of investment—well, at best, you guessed. If you did guess, you likely put in $1 million, or some multiple of $1 million. Whatever seems like lots.

If you do know the answer to both questions, congratulations. You are in a minority. Ask someone you know the same two questions, and if they can't answer them, give them this book. It will benefit them a lot more than you.

> *"Knowing where you're going is all you need to get there."*
> CARL FREDERICK

The point of this little exercise is just this—most of us don't have financial goals. We have wishes. Wishes don't work. Goals always work. That's a pretty big difference.

Most of us don't have a financial goal because we aren't looking for one. We aren't looking for one because of the best reason of all—we believe we already have one. This is dangerous. It's dangerous because of the fact that since we are convinced we *have* a financial goal, we feel it's a total waste of time to be reading books like this that tell us we *need* one. We want to hear about achieving the goal. How can I reduce taxes? How can I get a better return on my investments with less risk? How can I squeeze some savings out of an already stretched budget? These are the things everyone wants to hear about (and consequently they are the things that everyone writes about).

But the answers to these and the endless list of questions that sound like these are available ad nauseam. And they aren't difficult answers to comprehend. They are easy things to do. They work. Yet we, likely you in particular, aren't getting what we want!

Here's the reason. *We don't have a clearly defined goal.*

Here's what we do have:

TYPICAL LONG-TERM FINANCIAL "GOALS"

- I want lots of money.
- I want as much as I can get. (Sounds like lots to me.)
- I want as much as my rich friends.
- I want to keep what I have.
- I just don't want to run out of money before I run out of life.
- I just want enough to pay the bills.
- I want to pay less tax.
- I don't want to have to worry about money.

These aren't goals. These are just wishes, fears, and hopes that sound like goals. But they aren't goals. And they will be of *no* use in getting what you *really* want. Some of these statements more accurately describe what you *don't* want. What we really want to do is help you *decide* what you *do* want.

Goals must have four characteristics:

1. Goals must be specific and measurable.
2. Goals must be written down.
3. Goals must have a deadline.
4. Goals must reflect what you want—and be inspiring.

Let's look at each of these characteristics in more detail.

Goals Must Be Specific and Measurable

Let me turn the tables for a moment, and ask you to create a financial plan for me. I want to retire somewhere between 50 and 65, and I want to have lots of money. The first question is this. How much money do I need to accumulate?

> *"It is hard to begin to move when you don't know where you are moving, how to move, or if you are going to get there."*
>
> PETER VIVIO ZARLENGA

You need more information, don't you? Unless I tell you *exactly* what I want, which implies I have *decided* what I want, you can't even begin to work out the answer to my question!

OK, then, how about this. I want to have a gross income of $75,000 in today's dollars from my investments in 20 years. Assume an investment return of 9% and inflation of 3% per year over the next 20 years. Can you answer it now?

If you have a calculator you can determine that I would need $1,505,092 in 20 years. I can go from there to calculate how much I need to invest each month (what we *really* want to know) as well as a myriad of other things that will help us see that accumulating this sum is realistic and achievable. (*I will be using a Hewlett Packard 10B Business Calculator to work through examples. Results using other calculators or computer software may vary slightly.*)

From a purely logical perspective we can't do the math on things like big, lots and more. We *can* do the math on things like $1,000,000. It's specific, and measurable.

Goals which are in truth vague generalities, such as "I want to have more money," provide us with no sense of accomplishment because they are always out of reach. More implies more from any point. We get more, and still want more. With no destination, the goal soon takes on a futile appearance, and we give up. Our goals *must* be specific in order to create, and then stick with, plans to achieve them.

Goals Must Be Written Down

Your brain is a most amazing machine. Yet despite all that we know our brain does for us, scientists are certain that we are only utilizing a small fraction of its potential. That would suggest we can do *considerably* more than we are doing now.

You might think of your brain as you would a computer. Your brain has hardware—all the icky stuff that we can see and take x-rays of. And your brain has software—the programming that causes you to think the way you do. When we talk about neurons and nerve cells we are talking about the hardware. When we talk about your beliefs, your values, and your dreams, we are talking about the software, or the programming.

Our reflex responses are a good example of our brain's programming. If we see a flying object coming across the room at our head, we duck. Our brain is at work, saving us from a severe headache. We learn, quite young, that when we get hit, it hurts. Our brain stores this information and calls on it as needed, just as a computer stores and then later retrieves information to perform the various tasks it is called upon to do.

During our childhood we form beliefs about virtually everything. We form beliefs about what is right and what is wrong. We form beliefs about who we are, what we are good at, what we like and don't like, how to interact with others, and on and on. Much of what we learn, like ducking to avoid being hit, is important to our survival and well being. However, much of what we learn is actually limiting and self-defeating.

For example, as we grow up we form beliefs about our position in life. We may come to believe that we are "middle class," and furthermore we may believe that this means living in a nice house, having two children and a dog, driving a new car, and being perpetually in debt to pay for it all. We not only expect to have our version of a middle class life, we expect to *struggle* to have it. Our expectations form the self-fulfilling prophecy.

> *"We are what and where we are because we have first imagined it..."*
> DONALD CURTIS

Our beliefs form the basis of our programming and, ultimately, they give shape to our lives. We believe we will need to worry. And we do worry. We worry mostly about being unable to afford to stay in this middle-class life. No matter where we actually *are,* we always feel as though we are on the edge, as though the next problem will topple us into the socio-economic class below us. So we constantly have something to worry about. It's a vicious circle.

The essence of wanting to be rich is wanting to be free from worry about money. We have the power to do that by setting goals that give us exactly what we want. What we want will most certainly take us outside the belief structure we currently live in—outside our comfort zone. But our brain is deeply programmed to keep us *inside* this belief structure. So we need to reprogram our brain.

Wow, this *is* brain surgery!

Not quite. Your beliefs can be changed. Let's think of the simplest example—*The Little Engine Who Could.* Don't worry, I won't repeat the story—just the point. The Little Engine got up the hill when the big engine didn't because he *convinced* himself he could. He convinced himself by repeating to himself, "I think I can, I think I can."

When you set a goal, at some point, probably very soon, you will question your belief in that goal. If you set out to accumulate what you believe to be a *lot* of money in a short period of time there will be *many* days that you will think, "I can't do that!" If that goal is simply in the ether, or in your memory, it will soon get erased—replaced by the old goal, which might be something like "Hang on to what we have now." This goal is definitely believable since you've been achieving it quite nicely since birth.

If it is written down, however, you won't erase it or forget it. Furthermore, the act of writing your goal sends the message to your brain in another form. And the words on the page represent yet another way of reaching the brain with this message through the act of seeing it and reading it.

So, for example, we could write "$1,500,000 in 20 years." We can build mental images of what our life will look like when that goal is achieved. These new mental images will eventually replace the old images, or the old programming, that kept us struggling to achieve and maintain a middle-class existence. We should read our goal, and play these mental images over and over again. The repetition will create a new belief.

Goals need to be written down to elevate them beyond the level of mere wishes, past the New Year's Resolutions that are forgotten, and into the area of plans and commitments. They need to be written down so that they move out of our imagination, and into the world of reality.

Goals Must Have a Deadline

This seems self-evident. Without a deadline, a goal has no teeth. There is no need to take the first step, as there is no hurry to get to the destination. No motivation, and therefore no action. No action, and therefore no accomplishment.

The deadline also needs to be exact. If we set our sights on a range, say for example we decide to retire between the ages of 50 and 65, we will naturally revert to the "easier" goal, especially when pressed with more immediate needs that subjugate our long-term plans, like retirement. Set exact deadlines, or recognize that you have defaulted to your worst case-scenario.

Our deadlines also need to be believable. If you set your sights on accumulating $1,000,000 by Friday of this week, your mind can't comprehend how that could be possible, short of theft or winning a lottery. You can't believe it, and therefore it won't happen. If however you set your sights on accumulating $1,000,000 over the next 15 years, you can break it down into small steps, convince yourself it is achievable, and make it happen. Your growing belief as you move towards this goal will make it increasingly easier. (You may eventually adjust the goal to a higher amount or reach the goal sooner!)

So our goal, $1,500,000 in 20 years, has a specific, believable time frame. Put a year on it—in this case, 20 years from today. Now start crossing the days off on the calendar.

Goals Must Reflect What You Want—and Be Inspiring

If goals reflect what you really want, they *will* be inspiring. In fact, if you lose your zest for a goal you've set, ask yourself if that was what you really wanted. Especially in the case of financial matters, it's very important that this be well understood, primarily because it is never money that you want, yet money will be the way we both define and measure the ultimate goal.

> *"You return and again take the proper course, guided by what? —By the picture in mind of the place you are headed for…"*
> JOHN MCDONALD

What you want is what money provides. Your lifestyle, and your material needs and wants, are best *measured* in dollars and cents. But the substance is much more personal. This is the very essence of setting financial goals, and we will spend an entire chapter looking at it.

Our goal, $1.5 million in 20 years, is uninspiring when it stands alone. But when it is coupled with the underlying lifestyle that it promises, with a vision of all that can be done with the steady income stream that $1.5 million will produce, it should hold tremendous power to inspire. It is not the money, but what the money will be used for that will be our inspiration.

Greed is a powerful motivator, just like many other "negative" emotions—like hate and anger. But they never lead to happiness. If money is what you want, and you set out on an eternal quest to get more, and more, and more—ultimately getting the "biggest pile in the universe," then you shall likely get fairly rich. No—you will likely get "stinking" rich in most people's terms. That's not what I'm talking about here.

Most of us don't want the most money in the universe. We don't want to spend our lives on a quest for money. We don't even want to think about money. That's the key. We don't want to *think* about money—it's just that we have to. The bills come in, and what do you know, we need money to pay them. We need money for clothes, and for food. We need money to travel and take vacations. We need money to buy gifts, and to support our favourite causes. It goes on and on.

We want to have money, and spend money, and give money away. We just don't want to worry about it.

> "The indispensable first step in getting the things you want out of life is this: decide what you want."
> BEN STEIN

There is no greed associated with the notion I am putting forth. There is only a quest for self-fulfillment. And we cannot reach our true potential if we remain forever stuck on a treadmill of worry and angst over the money that seems to fuel everything we do.

Our society is filled with people who like rats on treadmills spend their entire lives worrying and striving for "more." They are on a ship with a destination unknown. There is nothing quite so worrisome, quite so feared, as the unknown.

There are a few, and you know some of them, who always know exactly where they are going. They constantly achieve more, and worry less. Their confidence may at times be mistaken for arrogance, and their lack of concern, especially about money, may seem careless. But they are universally envied. They understand one of the most important secrets of the universe. And you can too. It's simply this:

KNOW WHAT YOU WANT

Decide what this is. Decide what you want. Then set your course. The goal is already achieved.

> *"The first essential, of course, is to know what you want."*
> ROBERT COLLIER

SUMMARY OF KEY POINTS

The key to achieving or getting *anything* is to know exactly what it is that you want. Surprisingly, we seldom know *exactly*, especially in the case of financial planning.

We are often busy implementing a plan, when in fact we don't even know what the exact outcome of the plan is supposed to be.

We think we have goals, when often what we have are vague wishes, fears, and hopes.

Goals must have these four characteristics:

1. Goals must be specific and measurable.
2. Goals must be written down.
3. Goals must have a deadline.
4. Goals must reflect what you want—and be inspiring.

The secret to all your desires is simply this:
Know what you want.

ACTION STEP

If a genie popped out of a bottle right now, and asked you want you wanted, what would you say? You have three wishes. What are they? As you know, the genie insists that you be *specific*. Write your thoughts now, in the space overleaf, or in your journal.

2

WHY WE DON'T DO THE
ONE THING THAT MATTERS

"Nothing will ever be attempted
if all possible objections must first be overcome."
SAMUEL JOHNSON

A T this stage, virtually all books about financial planning move
on to the "how to" section. Reducing taxes, increasing yields,
asset allocation, reducing expenses, and those sorts of things. Not
that this isn't important stuff. It's just that without a clear, specific,
and inspiring goal, the black and white issues—the technical stuff—
do nothing more than give us a spot in the great money race. We
get all the tools we need to make comparisons.

Did your investments outperform those recently advertised in
the newspaper—you know—last year's top investments? Are your
mutual funds among the Top Ten funds of last year? Did you pay
too much tax? Is your mortgage rate too high? All of these questions,
and countless others we like to ponder, all point to *relative*
comparisons. In the end, they are meaningless.

Day to day and year to year there is only one question that we
should be repeatedly asking, and that is: "Am I taking the steps I
planned to take that will move me towards my goal?" Obviously,
we can't answer this question—in fact we won't even contemplate
asking the question—if we don't have a goal in mind. We need to

know the destination. In the exercise of retirement planning, there's only one destination, and only one opinion that matters—yours. It's *not* a race against the rest of the world. It's a journey that's carefully planned out.

Before we make assumptions about rates of return and analyze tax strategies, we need to know one thing—our target or destination. How much money, exactly, are we trying to accumulate, and when do we want to have it?

This isn't ground-breaking news. The word *goal* isn't something coined here. It's easy to do—really. And intuitively, we all know that it makes sense. We just don't do it. Why not?

Why don't we set *specific*, long-range financial goals?

Let's look at the "Top 9" reasons why we don't set specific retirement goals.

1. I don't believe goal-setting is all that important.
2. I don't want to be trapped inside a rigid plan.
3. I don't want to make sacrifices today.
4. I'm too old or too young.
5. I make a lot of money, or I don't make enough money.
6. I don't know how to set long-range goals.
7. Fear.
8. I just don't know what I want.
9. I don't have time.

Let's look at each of these reasons (excuses) for a moment. Pay particular attention to those that may strike a nerve.

I don't believe goal setting is all that important

Ah, the skeptic. A man who was much wiser (and richer) than I am, Henry Ford, said, *"Whether you think you can or think you can't—you are right."* In other words, I can't help you to believe. And you will prove yourself right regardless of which side of the debate you sit on.

Consider this tidbit of goal-setting trivia. A study was done at Harvard University in 1953. The students were surveyed to determine who had goals—written down. Only 3% of the students at Harvard in 1953 had goals written down. Twenty years later, in 1973, those 3% were worth more than the combined net worth of the other 97%. That's a remarkable testament to the power and importance of clearly defined goals. There's *plenty* more evidence.

The best advice I can give you is this. Read these three books: *Think & Grow Rich*, by Napoleon Hill, *Psycho-Cybernetics*, by Dr. Maxwell Maltz, and *The Seven Habits of Highly Effective People*, by Steven Covey. If these great works don't make you think twice about the importance of setting specific goals, certainly nothing I could say will either. If you read them and get hooked on the subject, call me, there are other similarly great books that you can read.

Am I suggesting that *all* financially secure, well-adjusted people have great financial goals? No. There are in fact many people who don't worry at all about their financial futures. They live in total confidence that they will always have more than enough and quite often that is because they have always *had* more than enough. They live within their means easily and effortlessly and they save regularly. They *have* goals, just not financial goals. In a sense, their beliefs allow

> *"A work well begun is half ended."*
> PLATO

21

them to transcend the financial goals. So in truth, they don't need them.

On the other hand, *most* people spend an inordinate amount of time worried about money. They struggle to live within their means, and find it difficult or impossible to save. They have no specific financial goals, but spend a great deal of time wishing for more money. These people will benefit enormously from the exercise of setting financial goals. By turning their wishes into goals, they give focus and direction to their day-to-day choices. All of the other issues, the details—like rates of return and taxes, can be calculated against the backdrop of the long-term target. Wishing is displaced by the realization of a plan.

If you set inspiring goals you can't help but take action. When your mind locks in on a target, the entire universe unleashes a chain of events to assist you. And very soon, stress is displaced by confidence.

It all starts with one decision.

I don't want to be trapped inside a rigid plan

Neither do I. Listen, we won't etch your goal in stone and hang it in the town square. You can change it, and you will—often. In fact, one of the most wonderful things that happens when you participate in personal goal setting, is that you eventually realize and understand the tremendous power inherent in your goals. Once you realize this, you begin to wonder why you didn't set your retirement goal higher! Of course, you can! So you will likely change your goal many times between now and retirement, and you will most likely always change it for the better!

> *"I am the master of my fate;*
> *I am the captain of my soul."*
> WILLIAM ERNEST HENLEY

The important thing is for you to agree that you don't want to be stuck where you are right now! One of the laws of nature is this: everything is either growing or dying. Nothing is standing still. You *can't* hold on to the life you have. You are either moving forward or backwards. Which way are *you* going?

The amazing thing is that it actually takes much less effort to move forward than it does to move backwards! Moving forward involves challenge, excitement, inspiration, teamwork, reward, achievement, accomplishment, fulfillment, and growth. Holding on, which means falling backwards, involves fear, concern, worry, pain, suffering, misery, failure, selfishness, and shame.

You pick.

I don't want to make sacrifices today

Getting something always involves giving up something else, doesn't it? Sacrifice. Pain. And most of us struggle with the idea of giving up something *now*, to get in return something *later*. What if I die tomorrow?

We are a society focused on the here and now. Yet our biggest *worry* remains tomorrow. Quite the paradox.

A man by the name of Sydney Harris put this paradox into perspective in a most succinct way. He said, *"The art of living successfully consists of being able to hold two opposite ideas in tension at the same time: first, to make long term plans as if we were going to live forever; and second, to conduct ourselves daily as if we were going to die tomorrow."*

Let me introduce another perspective. How much do you need to sacrifice today in order to accomplish your goal in the future? The fact is, very few know the answer. We assume we won't pay the price, and yet we have no idea what the price is. We don't even know what we might be paying the price for! In the absence of any information on the subject, we do nothing.

Obviously, doing nothing is *not* a good strategy. If nothing is what you are doing, it tends to be a great source of stress, since you know at the end of any given period of time you will continue to *have* nothing.

> *"Do the thing we fear, and the death of fear is certain."*
> RALPH WALDO EMERSON

Here's something to consider. Chances are you can't accurately account for all the money you spend monthly or annually. Even if you keep reasonable records, quite likely there is a sum of money that just "disappears" each month. We generally label this "miscellaneous" and chalk it up to minor items that we pay for in cash. But like a sock that disappears from the dryer, it remains a mystery.

Here's a sequel to this same mystery. Almost universally, when an individual decides to set aside a reasonable sum of money each month to invest, after a few months they say they don't notice it missing. It doesn't change their lifestyle or spending at all. Yes, this does seem to contradict the laws of our physical universe, and yet it is absolutely true. Try it.

Two points to make in summary. First, there will be both costs, and *benefits—immediately—*when we create a plan to achieve our long-term financial goal. Second, the cost won't be near as much as you think. Get an estimate.

I'm too old or too young

You're too old. OK then, let's find the line. When should you shut down all your hopes and dreams for the future and take all your marbles, put them in a safe place and spend the rest of your miserable days making sure you don't run out before you die? Some would have you believe age 65. I believe it's never.

First of all, we don't have the master plan for our lives, and therefore we don't know how long we will live. Some people die very young. Some live past 100.

Let's consider Emma, who is 75. She has $500,000 in investments. Her pension income is $25,000 annually and she only needs $30,000 to be very comfortable. She has more than enough. She doesn't need any goals. Does she?

Let's find out more. Emma does worry about money. She has five kids, and 12 grandchildren. She would like to leave *each of them* $100,000. But the half million, after taxes are deducted, will barely leave each of them $20,000. That's hardly a legacy. She would like to leave money to the lung association (her husband died of emphysema) and to her church. But can she do this and leave less to her children? And all her life she has longed to visit "the old country," but that would cost a lot of money, cutting deeper into her funds. Strangely, she even worries that if she lives too long, she herself might run out of money.

Why should a woman in Emma's financial position worry about money? She shouldn't. But, in the absence of a plan to realize her goals, she will continue to worry.

You see, she *does* have goals. Good ones. Goals that are inspirational, and worthy. She just hasn't asked for any help in setting a plan to quantify, prioritize, and then realize her goals.

> *"If I've got correct goals, and if I keep pursuing them the best way I know how, everything else falls into line. If I do the right thing right, I'm going to succeed."*
>
> DAN DIERDORF

Consequently, she sees them more as wishes. Wishes, you will recall, aren't helpful. In fact, they are often destructive. But they can be transformed into goals—goals possessing enormous power. The difference is belief. The fact is, she can do a lot more than she currently believes she can.

Should a 75-year-old woman (or man) have financial goals? There isn't a shred of doubt. Yes.

What about Larry and Susan, who are married and both 51? They would like to retire in 10 years, but are quite certain they won't be able to afford it. Larry will have a company pension, but he's uncertain exactly how much that will generate in income. They have about $250,000 combined in their RRSP plans, which they consider far too small for their station in life. Larry and Susan, like so many people, are convinced that they have done a poor job of managing their money up to now, and that it's far too late to salvage the life they dreamed of in retirement. When it comes to money, they will tell you that they are generally unhappy.

That can be turned around easily. They have the start of a powerful retirement goal—they already know *when* they want to retire. All they need to do is quantify the "how much" part, and build a strategy or plan to realize it. What they are overlooking at this point is the fact that their most productive saving years are in front of them. The house will soon be paid off, the kids are soon to leave home, and their incomes continue to rise. They can do a whole lot more in the next ten years than they realize—they've just never bothered to figure it out. When they do, they will find their relationship with money improves immensely.

It's always too late to change the past. It's always the perfect time to change the future. And this leads us perfectly into the other half of this "age" debate. I'm too young!

This is one we've heard a lot about. The standard answer in the industry revolves around the fact that if you put $10,000 into the ABC Mutual Fund the day you were born, by the time you were 50 you would own most of the western world. But if you wait until you are 50 to put that $10,000 into the ABC Mutual Fund you would have, well, $10,000, which after being adjusted for inflation won't buy you a *map* of the western world.

This is true (although slightly exaggerated). Time is a key component in creating wealth. The more the better. Start young and put time on your side. But there is an even more significant rebuttal to this objection.

Really, this excuse boils down to simple procrastination. "I'm too young" sounds a whole lot better than "I'll do it later," but it ends up being the same thing. Procrastination is a habit. And like all habits, it's a tough habit to break.

> *"Habit is either the best of servants or the worst of masters."*
> NATHANIEL EMMONS

Habits and goals are intricately linked. We naturally develop habits that move us in the direction of our goals. If you set a long-range financial goal, and get emotionally involved with that goal, you will *have* to do something about it! Anything! Your quest to realize the goal will force your mind and body to take action. It's that simple. And, you will develop positive habits. Habits that will ensure the realization of your goal.

Say you are 12, and your allowance is $4 per week. Too young, right? No! Twelve-year-olds may have trouble setting goals for retirement, but they can probably get excited about saving for a new CD, a baseball glove, or a special gift! Save 50 cents per week. You are now moving towards your goal. Plus, you have developed a very positive habit. And habits, bad and good, are hard to break.

It doesn't matter how old you are. You are not too old, and you are not too young. If you are thinking about this (and you are, aren't you, because you're reading this) then the perfect time is now.

I make a lot of money, or I don't make enough money

Sadly, many believe that setting financial goals and accumulating wealth is something only the "middle class" can or should do. And if we define ourselves as middle class, then we shift this belief to the "upper-middle class," or some other segment of the class which excludes us. Or we just feel guilty about not doing it.

In truth, setting goals has *nothing* to do with where you are starting, and everything to do with where you want to end up.

Let's start by looking at the high-income side of this excuse.

The Millionaire Next Door, by Thomas J. Stanley, Ph.D., and William D. Danko, Ph.D., is a most revealing look into the millionaires in the U.S. And one of the discoveries was this: high-income earners have no greater chance of becoming "wealthy" than do middle- or even low-income earners. What they repeatedly found was that many high-income earners also have disproportionately high consumption habits. Conversely, many people who appear to live fairly routine middle class lives, have gobs of money—they just don't spend it!

The high-income earner has an unusual but very dangerous trap to avoid. High-income earners already *feel* wealthy. They live in the best neighbourhoods, drive the best cars, wear the latest fashions, and belong to the best clubs. In the opinion of many they *are* the rich!

Not necessarily. When you think about it, a high-consumption lifestyle requires an ongoing high income. When the working income stops (and someday it will) it must be replaced by a similarly high income from financial assets. A bigger pot, if you will. Are these people accumulating a pot big enough to sustain their lifestyle? In the vast majority of cases, they are no better at this than those in other income categories.

Don't get me wrong here, I am not condemning those who like the "high life." I'm just sounding the bell to warn that a high income does not even remotely negate the need for long-term goals and plans. In this department, we are all the same.

Let's go to the opposite extreme—"I don't make enough money." Well, you could just read the last section backwards. It's kind of the same thing, but in reverse. If you live happily on a lower income today, then you may simply aspire to be assured the same income in the future.

As an aside, if you think your income is *too* low, you should be thinking of ways to fix that. There are plenty of options. And, in fact, this book is about planning *anything*, which of course includes finding a career that is more financially rewarding. Do it. Then reread the "I make a lot of money" section again.

Anyhow, if your financial requirements aren't in the same league as the Rockefellers (are they still around?) that really doesn't make a bit of difference. You still need a pot of money, to keep the same (or desired) cash flow going when you stop working. It's just going to be a smaller pot!

This stuff is starting to get simple, isn't it?

I don't know how to set long range goals

Good news. The next chapter is your guide to setting a financial goal. If this is your only excuse, you've just run out of excuses.

Fear

While fear is admittedly a powerful motivator, it is never inspiring. If fear is your primary reason for doing *anything*, your life is probably *not* going in the general direction you want it to.

Fear around money manifests itself in a great number of ways. In fact, probably everything else on this list could be reduced to some sort of fear. Fear of being wrong, fear of commitment, fear of responsibility or accountability, fear of giving up something, fear of making a mistake, fear of loss, fear of failure.

The kind of fear that is not already on this list, but is nonetheless very real, is simply fear of money itself.

Most people don't come right out and say "money scares me," but by saying a host of other things, that's what they really mean. They say things like "I don't like risk," or "I hate paying taxes," or "I don't want to know about this, you just do what you think is best." What they are really saying is, "Money scares me."

Many financial advisors and other professionals revel in (and profit from) the intricate complexities that when woven together form our financial system. The tax laws and acts of legislation dealing with investments, banks, trust companies, insurance companies, corporations, etc., become more complicated with each new act of parliament. Lawyers and accountants can barely keep up, let alone the average citizen.

Indeed, our money system is complex, and more than a little scary. But listen carefully to this. Understanding how an automobile works is complex, but driving one is simple. In the same way, our money system is complex, *but* creation of wealth is simple.

> *"Our life is frittered away by detail…Simplify, Simplify."*
> HENRY DAVID THOREAU

So simple in fact, that any idiot can do it (and some have). Quite often, getting caught in the trappings of fancy financial dealings that wind precariously through the complex tax laws *prevents* wealth creation. Conversely, simple steps, taken along a simple road that is well understood, *create* wealth almost effortlessly.

Don't let the financial press and the financial services industry convince you that the complexities of money have moved beyond you. All you *really* need to know is what you want it to do for you.

I just don't know what I want

Actually, this is a pretty good excuse, and perhaps the most common. But it begs an obvious rebuttal. If you don't know what you want, is it then your fate to accept whatever life hands you?

Discovering what you want is no small task. This isn't a matter to be resolved by spending a few quiet hours alone. And you can't get someone else to tell you what you want; you need to discover it for yourself.

"What do I want?" is both the biggest question and the smallest question. The answer ultimately encompasses everything in your world, yet it involves no one but yourself.

> *"We find what we expect to find, and we receive what we ask for."*
> ELBERT HUBBARD

The sheer size of this undertaking and the solitude of this quest perhaps combine to make this appear to be the most formidable of tasks. Couple that with the vast array of fears that this question conjures up, and you have a lifetime of soul-searching, contemplation, and idealizing that comes with a healthy dose of worry, frustration, and angst. It's easy to make this a spiral of non-committal.

In short, it's easy not to decide anything in an effort to make your decision perfect.

This remarkable and important journey, however, can be initiated with one easy step. Decide on *something*. Anything really. Just decide.

You most surely do not know exactly what you want in every aspect of the rest of your life. Many of the things you will one day do or one day own aren't yet even a part of our collective imagination. But within the scope of your present reality, you are currently accepting in your life a great deal of "stuff" that you *don't* want. There's only one way to get rid of that, and that's by turning your attention towards that which you *do* want.

Let me remind you of the second point on this list—your goals aren't going to be carved in stone. But by choosing from the current options that which you want the most, you set your course towards discovering things you will want even more. You will stop floating aimlessly, and start moving forward with intent.

> *"Nothing happens unless first a dream."*
> CARL SANDBURG

Remember, Columbus had an entirely different goal in mind when he left the shores of Spain. But he had a very specific goal, and he accomplished much more than he could ever have imagined.

I don't have time

This is the universal excuse of our era. Ironically, all of the modern technology that was supposed to create a four-day workweek and tons of leisure time has done just the opposite. We are so wired into our work lives, with cell phones, pagers, the internet, and whatever comes next, that we are now capable of working literally around the clock. Sadly, that's exactly what many do.

Most of the time (but not always) this is done for the sake of money. And herein lies the entire point of this book.

Stop for a minute, right now, and ask yourself these questions. If my job or career didn't earn me any money, would I keep doing it? Money is an important part of why we work so hard, isn't it?

How much money am I working for? Careful now, you aren't allowed to answer with vague generalities such as "As much as I can get," or "I'll know when I have enough," or "Lots more than I have

now." Think about it. What do you *really* want? If money were not
a factor, if you had an endless supply, what would you do? Where
would you go? How would you live? How much time would you
spend with loved ones? Who would you spend your time with?

These are not easy questions to
contemplate because they ask us to
let go of our belief that we are bound
and limited by our money supply. In
truth we aren't, and we only realize
that when we ask these kinds of
questions and search for the answers.

> "*Every body continues
> in its state of rest,
> or of uniform motion
> in a right line,
> unless it is compelled
> to change that state
> by forces impressed upon it.*"
>
> SIR ISAAC NEWTON

Your life should be, and can be,
focused on the things you want to do
with your money, not on the way you
will acquire it! Think of how
wonderful your life could be if it weren't for the stress and strain of
earning and keeping money!

Your life could change dramatically if you would devote a few
hours or days getting your sights set on the life you want. Is it
worth a little of your time?

I like to think of our personal financial goal in the same way a
charitable organization, for example, a hospital, might think of a
fundraising effort. If the hospital needs $1,000,000 to buy an
important piece of equipment they will proudly build a plan around
that precise goal—raise $1,000,000—and then buy the equipment.
They will set a deadline, and create a plan involving various
fundraising activities to achieve the goal. And almost always they
post a big sign somewhere—you've seen them—with a thermometer
on the sign. At the top of the thermometer will be the stated goal—
$1,000,000. Notice that the top won't name the piece of
equipment—which isn't as measurable. And the thermometer will

be graduated, probably in $100,000 increments. Then they will fill in, usually in red, the amount of money raised to date, to show the entire world the goal, and the progress to date.

It may also be important to emphasize here that the hospital isn't trying to raise cash just to have it lying around. They have a specific, and important, use for that money. It's not the desire to see the hospital have $1,000,000 that gets so many people to commit cash to the project. It's the desire to see the hospital have the new *whatsit* that is going to help them save lives. That's a worthy goal, and we line up to help what we consider to be worthy causes.

Your personal financial goal is no less important. Make yourself a thermometer. And get out your red marker—because it's going to start filling up.

> *"You will become as small as*
> *your controlling desire;*
> *or as great as*
> *your dominant aspiration."*
> JAMES ALLEN

SUMMARY OF KEY POINTS

There are a number of supposedly legitimate excuses that prevent us from setting financial goals. The most common are:

1. I don't believe goal setting is all that important.
2. I don't want to be trapped inside a rigid plan.
3. I don't want to make sacrifices today.
4. I'm too old or too young.
5. I make a lot of money, or I don't make enough money.
6. I don't know how to set long range goals.
7. Fear.
8. I just don't know what I want.
9. I don't have time.

All of these excuses, and others, will only serve to stop us from getting what we really want.

ACTION STEP

From the list above, circle the "excuse" that you identify with the most. (You may circle more than one.) Now reread the section dealing with that excuse. In the space below, write a statement affirming your new belief about this excuse in the form of a goal. For example, if you previously did not believe that goal setting was important, you may write something like *I know that setting clear, concise, inspiring goals is essential, and I will have a*

specific financial / retirement goal determined and written down by...
**Make your own thermometer. Leave the goal at the
top of the stem blank until you have finished the book.**

_____

_____

_____

_____

_____

_____

_____

_____

_____

_____

_____

_____

_____

_____

_____

_____

_____

_____

_____

_____

_____

_____

_____

_____

_____

3

CREATING YOUR
RETIREMENT VISION

"Nothing happens unless first a dream."
CARL SANDBURG

A LL right, so we need to have financial goals. Good enough, let's scribble some on a piece of paper and get on with the good stuff—you know, lowering taxes, increasing yields, that sort of thing.

Sorry, but it's not that easy. First we have to figure out how to arrive at these all-important, meaningful goals. Where do they come from?

Dr. Stephen Covey's landmark book *The Seven Habits of Highly Successful People* is truly a handbook for our time. And the second of his seven habits (I really think it should be the first) is *"Begin with the end in mind."*

To begin with the end in mind so perfectly encapsulates what this chapter is all about, that it almost seems pointless to do anything other than to send you away to read this section of Dr. Covey's book, and continue when you return. However, despite the fact that this book has been so widely read, and despite the fact that the connection between his fundamental idea and the notion of setting a retirement goal is so obvious, it seems to elude many of us. Let's explore this further.

First and foremost, it is important to establish that setting your retirement goal does not, indeed cannot, begin with picking a really big number to shoot for. It's easy to do this and to somehow feel that the exercise is complete. The experts will tell you that you need 70% of your current income in retirement. If you accept this as fact, then a technician merely needs to know when you want to retire, the assumed rate of inflation, and your anticipated return on investments. Out will pop a magic, and very important, number. (More on this in Chapter 4.) But something very important has been overlooked. *Accumulating a sum of money is not the end.*

In fact, accumulating a sum of money is more accurately the *beginning* of retirement. The end is death. What's important, of course, is that time in between.

Choosing a specific time, and a specific amount of money to accumulate, is setting the goal, and it is extremely important. In getting to this goal, however, something else is needed. A vision.

> *"Think and feel yourself there! To achieve any aim in life, you need to project the end-result. ... Think of the elation, the satisfaction, the joy! Carrying the ecstatic feeling will bring the desired goal into view."*
> GRACE SPEARE

When the hospital sets out to raise a million dollars to buy a new piece of life-saving equipment, their goal is the million dollars. Their vision is saving lives. When you set out to pay off your mortgage, your goal is $0 owing, but your vision is freedom from debt and from the monthly payments that debt entails. When a young student sets out to earn a law degree his goal is the LLB, but his vision is a fulfilling career.

Your goal may be to accumulate $1.5 million by age 60. Your vision is what you will do from that point forward. What *will* you do when you retire?

This question—what will you do when you retire—has enormous power. This question can and will help us to tap into the most potent source of power at our disposal—our imagination. During the past century our focus has been on exploring the far reaches of our physical world and even our physical universe. But recently, our focus has shifted inward. The greatest journey of exploration underway now is a journey to the depths of our own minds.

Bookstores attest to this progressive shift—call it an evolution. Books that search our minds, our souls, our emotions, and our understanding of spirituality consistently dominate the best-seller list. The immensely popular *Celestine Prophecy* is a good example.

The message coming loud and clear from currently divergent but rapidly converging sources is that our lives unfold as we imagine them. Our thoughts literally give shape to our reality. Whatever we *believe* is our truth. And most importantly, we can therefore change our outer world by changing our thoughts.

> *"We are what we think.*
> *All that we are arises*
> *with our thoughts.*
> *With our thoughts,*
> *we make our world."*
> GAUTAMA BUDDHA

The message isn't new, but it's coming to us more frequently, and from more of the mainstream sources, and we are starting to understand it. And as we gain understanding of the power we already possess, we can then finally use it.

Giving up the old understanding isn't easy. We cling to the old familiar paradigm. In some way it seems almost easier to believe that life happens to us, that we must work with whatever we are given, and that we are powerless to change our destiny.

A wonderful aspect of retirement planning is that it stands at the crossroads of the old and new paradigms. It calls on us to create a *vision* of our future. Then it helps us to use the tools of the old paradigm, the *practical* path of achievement, to convince us that our vision is achievable and show us the physical steps we need to take. When some aspect of your future vision calls for something you presently deem to be impossible, like being able to fly, a financial plan can be constructed that will show you the ladder that already exists in our physical world which will take you there—one step at a time.

In a world in which money is often given the same level of importance as air, retirement planning may be one of the most important catalysts in helping us to move beyond our current level of understanding, and into a new understanding of prosperity consciousness.

This is powerful stuff—perhaps not what you expected to find in a book about financial planning. But check your emotions. If you are feeling excited right now, you know these ideas have the potential to ignite your dreams, and to change your life.

Let's get back to this life-changing question then. What will you do when you retire? Notice that we are asking what *will* you do, and not what do you *want* to do. (This exercise is all about gaining confidence and *believing*. Select your words accordingly.)

> *"All of our dreams can come true—if we have the courage to pursue them."*
> WALT DISNEY

The answers to this question will create a fairly clear distinction between two polarized groups. On one hand, there are those who will answer based on the limitations of their present circumstances. For the most part they will imagine doing in retirement more of what they are doing now, with more time to "rest and relax." These are people who approach retirement planning from an orientation of lack. They are the "have-nots." They see money as a zero-sum game. There is only so much to go around, and someone else has some of theirs. They worry most about not being able to maintain the status quo in retirement. They will probably not want to project a retirement date any earlier than age 65, and they will *hope* that their disposable income will be roughly the same as it is today.

In the other camp are those who, at the extreme, may be characterized as dreamers. They will project a retirement lifestyle much better than the lifestyle they live today. They will be much more prone to projecting an earlier retirement date, such as age 50, and will likely see their retirement income as higher than their current income. This group sees the world from an orientation of abundance and that is how they approach retirement planning. They are the "haves." They believe money is in unlimited supply, and not a zero-sum game.

Both of these groups can and will realize their respective visions. The question is, which vision is more compelling and more inspiring? I hope the answer is obvious.

Whether you have an *abundance mentality* or a *lack mentality* is not merely determined by your current station in life or your current or future income levels. It's an attitude. It's a belief system. In our current paradigm of money, we build plans that fit our perspective. We have the tools now, and an understanding that will allow us to plan for the future we *want*, and allow our perspective to adjust.

The real point of differentiation between these two groups is fear. Those who approach life from a perspective of lack, approach retirement planning from a basis of fear. Those who approach life from a perspective of abundance, see nothing to fear. Those who fear, think, "If I don't plan for my retirement and accumulate lots of money, I'll probably end up working forever, or eating cat food, or living on the streets" and so on.

While it may appear that I am suggesting here that these two groups are completely distinct, it is in fact more of a continuum. Most of us, if not all, fall somewhere in between. All of us harbour some feelings of lack, and suffer from various levels of fear. And unfortunately, it feels as though the entire world is trying to ignite and then fan the flames of that fear. If it's fear you want, there are plenty of "experts" willing to serve it up.

There are three legs to the stool of fear when it comes to retirement planning. One, we are living longer—a lot longer if the statistics bear any truth. If you were born in 1900 you had a life expectancy of 45. A child born in 1996 is expected to live to 83. So someone born in 1900 really didn't even expect to retire, and today we expect to spend 18 years or more in retirement. As these projections lengthen (and it's common today for people to plan on living until age 90) the price tag of retirement increases dramatically.

The second leg of the fear stool is demographics. In Canada, our retirement social net is a pay-as-you-go plan. Those who are retired and collecting the Canada Pension Plan are receiving the funds from those of us still working. Currently there are five working Canadians supporting every retired Canadian. But here come the baby boomers—a large generation who are also living longer. As the boomers start to retire in 2010, and more of them retire each year, this support system will collapse. By 2015 there will only be three working Canadians supporting every retired Canadian. The five-to-one ratio is already a strain, so realistically the current Canada Pension Plan system cannot continue without radical change.

The third leg of the fear stool is lack of preparedness. We *know* retirement is coming. In fact we *hope* we will make it to retirement and that we can actually stop working. And yet we aren't doing much about it. One survey recently conducted by *Manulife Financial* showed that 83% of Canadians thought it was important to have a financial plan, but sadly, only 39% said that they had one.

Scary stuff indeed. But don't despair.

To see the world through a perspective of abundance, means to see the future based on positive change. When you believe that you positively impact the future, you realize that the problems we see today

> "It may be those who do most, dream most."
> STEPHEN LEACOCK

are merely problems to solve, not problems to cave in to. When one looks at retirement from a *positive* perspective it becomes an exercise in opening up possibilities. It is an exercise in realizing dreams. It's inspiring. It's motivating. It changes—by improving—your life immediately.

In order to accept retirement planning from this perspective, we need to get past the fear. That's what retirement planning is really all about. Making it real. Making it possible. And proving that your fears are unfounded.

Let's look again at the three legs of our stool of fear, from a perspective of optimism and abundance.

Life expectancy. Isn't it incredible that some financial wizards have managed to take such an inspiring fact and turn it into a negative? We are living longer! Hurrah for medical science! Hurrah for our changing attitudes towards good health, proper diet, exercise, and preventative maintenance! Really now, this is a *good* thing isn't it!

How about demographics? The baby boomers have pushed the limits of everything they've touched, and that will surely continue. Hospitals were overcrowded when they were born. Schools were overcrowded when they showed up for kindergarten. Universities were surprised when they showed up there in large numbers. The job market was certain not to support their large numbers when they graduated. On it goes.

Yet the boomers not only survive, they thrive. They are the best-educated generation ever. They represent the lion's share of our leadership in the new millennium. They've led the way in changing forever how we live and do business, through the current technological revolution. Let's not bring out the violins just yet.

> *"We have forty million reasons for failure, but not a single excuse."*
> RUDYARD KIPLING

Really, the third leg is the one that will cause the stool to collapse and our fears to dissipate. It's a pretty weak leg to begin with. If our only concern remains that we are ill-prepared for retirement, then—get ready for this solution—*let's get prepared!* There's no one else to blame here, and no one to turn to for help. It's up to us. It's up to you.

When we overcome fear we begin to see money for what it truly is—a man-made device to keep score. Nothing more. We are then free to approach life from a perspective of abundance. From the abundance viewpoint, our future is without limit. But our future is our *responsibility*.

This is an important point. From the perspective of fear, or lack, we hope that a fair society will ensure that our needs our met, and that our fair share is provided to us. From the perspective of abundance we can have whatever we want—but we alone must decide what that is. You must decide on the course of action to attain your goals, and you must accept responsibility for the choice you made.

The responsibility here entails being happy with your choices, and not complaining. There's no one else to blame. This responsibility involves initiating change. It involves committing to a plan, and taking action. This kind of responsibility is not something that everyone rushes to embrace. This may explain to a great degree why there are so few who are truly wealthy.

Consider my clients, Maggie and Peter. They have a decent combined income and live within their means, but they had not managed to accumulate much in the way of savings. More importantly, they were renting their home, and seemed convinced that owning a home was beyond their reach. They believed in abundance, just *not* for them. They were almost resigned to renting forever and wanted to focus on saving for retirement, hoping not to fail in that department as well.

Their retirement *vision* included owning a home. The retirement plan they wanted to pursue did not. After some discussion, we designed a plan which included buying a home *now*. They were definitely scared, but excited and, more importantly, inspired. *This* plan was getting them what they truly wanted. And with the numbers in front of them, saying it could be done, they had to admit they were starting to believe.

They adjusted their thinking a little, and their budget a little. They bought the house. Interestingly, they suddenly found themselves able to save more than they expected. In a meeting recently Maggie said to me, "I don't know what you did, but we seem to have more money now, although I know we don't, and we most certainly don't worry about money like we used to!"

Although Maggie wondered if I deserved some of the credit for their newfound relationship with money, the real credit belongs to them. They made a decision with respect to what they wanted and, more importantly, they took responsibility for getting it.

If you find yourself generally experiencing thoughts of lack and feelings of fear, retirement planning can, and should, help you to open an important door. By giving shape to your own unique retirement dreams and then planning, within the boundaries of your present circumstances, to realize them, you take a bold step into responsibility for your own future.

You may, for example, create a plan that assumes you will receive no government benefits in retirement, as many younger people do, and by doing so you can see how *freedom* is a most achievable goal. (While assuming the total collapse of our social system is decidedly negative, taking total responsibility for your own financial well-being is an important step.)

If you find yourself already believing that abundance is the truth, then retirement planning is one of the most important tools you will find to harness the immense power that lies within you.

Either way, let's imagine that you are building a house. You have before you all the tools and supplies you need. But you have no plan. You aren't sure what the house is supposed to look like when it's finished. You could, I suppose, start with the obvious things—dig a hole for the foundation (but how big?) and lay the blocks. But it would be a struggle, wouldn't it? And the house may not turn out as well as you'd like.

Now imagine that you have a plan. You have the blueprints. You have a picture of the finished product, with step-by-step instructions on how to build the house. This is much easier, and more likely to end with the desired result, isn't it?

Such is the case with retirement planning. We need to know what our finished product should look like, and we need to know the steps to get there. Most importantly, we want to know the next step. That requires a plan. And the plan requires you to answer the question—*What am I building?* That's the vision.

And so, as we go in search of our retirement goal, we must first determine our retirement vision. We must answer the question, *What will I do when I retire?*

In answering this question, don't project yourself into old age. That will only serve to put limits on what you perceive you can or should do. Answer the question in this way: "If I retired today, with all the money I needed, what would I do?"

Offering help here borders on influencing, and it is important—extremely important—that you realize the answer to this question is completely unique to you. It should be influenced by only one thing—your heart's desire.

But, to fuel your imagination, consider a list of things such as these:

- Travel—where, how, why?
- Recreation—golf, tennis, shuffle board, skiing, watersports?
- Writing a book.
- Volunteering to help a favourite charity.

> *"Visualize this thing you want. See it, feel it, believe in it. Make your mental blue print, and begin to build!"*
> ROBERT COLLIER

- Crafts and hobbies—sewing, painting, woodworking, sculpting.
- Theatre—as a performer or audience member?
- Working—the dream job you don't pursue now because of money!
- Exploring and learning—what subjects interest you?
- More time devoted to your church or faith.
- Education—what do you wish you had studied?
- Cottage—summer or winter home?

Make *your own* list. Add description to the items on your list. Be as specific as you can possibly be—as if you were creating a shopping list for someone else to go out and bring you the exact things you want.

For example, *I* might say that I want to travel with the pro golfing tour, taking in two stops on the tour every year, staying in the same hotel as the pros and watching every round. I want to see different courses and different parts of the world on every stop. And I want to do this from the time I turn 55 for as long as my health allows. Hey, I'm getting kind of excited by this talk!

Let's make the picture more vivid. I can imagine the feel of the grass on the great golf courses of the world. I can hear the quiet of a putt being lined up, and the sudden roar of the crowd when the ball drops into the hole. I can imagine walking into the hotel lobby, seeing one of my favourite players, stopping to chat and getting yet another autograph in my journal.

You see, while goals are cold hard facts, visions are living pictures that you can see, hear, taste, and touch. The more vivid the vision, the more inspiring your goals will be. And the more likely you will be to get *exactly* what you want. When the picture becomes so real to you that you can see it, hear it, taste it, and feel it, it's hard to resist. Other things will diminish in importance, and rightly so. What you truly want will take the stage, and you will have it, faster than you imagine.

Once all of your retirement vision is in place (my golf-trip example is obviously just part of the year...there's more work to do!) It's relatively easy to quantify it. A travel agent can help me with the golfing tour, for example. Then it's time to generate a plan to have sufficient funds to realize the dream. Really, that's the easy part.

This exercise is calling on us to take the most important, and possibly shortest, bit of advice ever dispensed—"Know thyself." These words are credited to Socrates, although many have uttered the same thing. These words appeared over the entrance to the ancient temples in Rome, as they were believed by the Romans to be the secret to all that was possible in the universe. Today, these words hang over the imaginary doorways of our minds, as we travel inward on a journey to discover what it is we truly want, and how our desires can be effortlessly fulfilled.

It may seem to some that retirement planning is just an exercise in math and finance. It may seem to some that retirement planning is just one more path to disappointment and frustration as one discovers unfulfilled desires.

But for those who engage, truly engage, in the exercise of planning retirement, they immediately engage in the exercise of changing present circumstances.

Based on the tools at your disposal, and your perception of the immediate future, you will build a plan to realize your dreams. You will turn them into goals. But as you move

> "We all go where our vision is."
> JOSEPH MURPHY

forward, taking each step on the plan as outlined, new tools will come to light. As you grow, new understandings will sharpen your awareness of opportunities that exist to realize and even accelerate your plan. And the universe will unleash all of its power in order to assist you.

Consequently, your vision of the future will change—it will improve. Gradually, the dream you held for retirement will become the reality you experience today. You simply cannot set your heart on something, work to achieve it, and not have it happen. You won't wait thirty years. It will happen sooner. Just get your heart *set* on a new car, or a trip to a tropical island, or whatever, and you'll see what I mean.

This then is what is meant by "decide what you want."

First, you must know who you are. You must determine, based on your unique desires, what you most want to be, what you most want to have, and what you most want to do. You can't do this by leafing through catalogues or watching others. You have to look within. You must strive to "Know thyself." This is the key to your vision.

Once you have made that decision, then you must accept responsibility to fulfill your vision, and realize your dream. Deciding means believing. Believing in yourself. Believing in your dreams. Taking responsibility means allowing the inspiration to move you to action.

> *"If one advances confidently in the direction of his dreams, and endeavors to live the life which he has imagined, he will meet with a success unexpected in common hours."*
> HENRY DAVID THOREAU

Think of the hospital again. The hospital wants to raise $1 million. But the fact is they really don't want the money at all. What they want is the new equipment that *costs* $1 million. This new machine will save more lives. Maybe the life of someone you know. Maybe yours. Inspiring isn't it.

If the hospital sought the money so that the administration staff could get a raise, they would not succeed. What makes fund-raising efforts so successful is that they have inspiring visions attached to the goal. Visions that can capture the hearts of thousands of people.

Your vision only needs to capture one heart. Yours.

If money is involved in the realization of your inspiring vision, and generally it is, get a calculator, a computer, or a financial advisor. Now you need to crunch some serious numbers.

SUMMARY OF KEY POINTS

- To be effective, and powerful, goals need to come from a vision—a compelling vision of your future.
- The message getting louder and clearer today is this—our thoughts literally shape our reality.
- The question is, "What will you do when you retire?"
- Retirement planning should help us to see past our fears and believe in our dreams.
- Create a vivid picture of the life you want.
- The best advice of all is this: "Know thyself."

ACTION STEPS

If money were unlimited, what would you do? Where would you live? What would you own? Who would you help? Formulate a vision of your retirement that encompasses your answers. Don't let money restrict your thinking. This exercise is about the future and about dreams—big dreams. Paint a vivid picture. Use descriptive language. Write in the first person, present tense.

Read **Stephen Covey's** *The Seven Habits of Highly Effective People.*

4

DOING THE MATH

"Do the thing, and you'll have the power."

RALPH WALDO EMERSON

IF you skipped ahead to this chapter in an attempt to get to the "how to" section of the book, let me tell you two important things. First, the steps outlined here may prove to be a little sketchy for you—you might be disappointed. Second, and more importantly, this is probably the least important section of the entire book.

A better understanding of the mathematics involved in the world of finance is certainly helpful. If nothing else, it will at least help you to carry on an intelligent conversation with your financial advisor. But in the end, this is the stuff you can get someone else, or even a machine, to do for you. It's truly the easy stuff. It can be as simple as writing a cheque. I know what you're saying. I shouldn't use the words math and simple in the same paragraph. Actually, that's a good place to start.

Think back to your secondary school days. What was your *least* favourite subject? A fair number of you will answer math. I know, I was a secondary school math teacher.

Teachers refer to it as math anxiety. And one of the best tools that teachers have to help students overcome it is money. No, I don't mean paying students to learn their algebra. I mean using money to illustrate mathematical principles.

Strangely enough, the same student who has difficulty solving the equation $3x + 2x = 25$, can tell you in a jiffy that if you have 3 bills and he has 2 bills and they total $25, then they are $5 bills. Money is one way—perhaps the best way—to bring numbers and math to life.

So for the most part, although we may have struggled with algebra and geometry, we graduate knowing how to handle money. We know how much change to expect when we make a purchase at the store, and we can calculate our take-home pay by applying our tax rate and subtracting other deductions.

Then along comes someone with a new investment idea that involves futures contracts, derivatives, discount values, covered call options, or something sounding very sophisticated. Your eyes glaze over just like they did when the grade 11 math teacher was trying to explain factoring a polynomial. This is different though. Back in grade 11 you were pretty sure that factoring a polynomial wasn't going to come up in your day-to-day life, but these investment strategies may in fact be important to your financial well-being. Now you begin to wish you'd paid more attention in math class.

Here's the good news. It doesn't need to be—in fact it shouldn't be—complicated. In this department, simpler is always better. Furthermore, there is an abundance of great help in this area.

Consider your car. You definitely want to know how to drive it. That's why you have a car. But you don't necessarily want to know how to build it, or even fix it. There are people to do that. It can, however, prove valuable to have a reasonable understanding of how the car works. For example, if you go to your mechanic and he tells you that your *thingamajig* is shot and it's going to cost $3,298 to repair it, you feel pretty uncomfortable when you realize you have no idea what a *thingamajig* is, or what it does. Can you still drive the car without it? Should you get a new one, or find a used one?

Should you buy a new car instead? We worry about the legitimacy of expensive auto repairs, largely because we can't validate the work within our own understanding. We spend large sums on auto repairs, simply because we trust the mechanic.

The purpose of the next few pages is to give you a sense of how to quantify your retirement goals and turn them into action plans for today. This information won't turn you into a financial advisor, but it will make you more comfortable speaking with a financial advisor and reviewing the plan that you prepare together. Or, if you are a do-it-your-selfer, it will help you make some sense of the many programs currently available to help you get this job done.

Actually, there are very comprehensive, easy to use software packages available today that make crunching the numbers a thing of the past. To illustrate the mechanics and simplify the process, I will do all calculations using my HP 10B calculator. (Once again let me point out that your answers may vary slightly depending on the calculator or planning tool that you use.)

Let's get on with it then.

What we want to do here is find the specific answer to a very important question. How much money do you need in order to retire, when you want to retire, in the style you imagine? By determining exactly how much you need, we can then determine exactly what you must do between now and then in order to realize your retirement vision. The answer to this question—this number—becomes an important retirement *goal*.

There are six factors or variables which will influence the retirement goal:

1. Future income needs
2. Inflation
3. Years until retirement

4. Income tax rate
5. Life expectancy
6. Rate of return on investments.

These aren't ranked in order of importance. I put them in this order because it tends to be the most logical way to approach these issues, with one generally leading us into a discussion of the next.

Changing any one of these variables will change the retirement goal—in some cases dramatically. So it's important that we understand the implications of the values we use in these variables, and choose according to our unique personalities, and our beliefs.

Three of these factors offer only limited choice, and virtually no future control. Those are inflation, income tax rate, and life expectancy. We can choose to use different assumptions, but we ultimately don't have much influence over the actual results. We can assume a rate of inflation, but we don't control what it will actually be. We can apply an assumed tax rate, but unless you are the Prime Minister, the tax rate is going to be determined by others. And you can assume that you will live to be 95, but other than looking after your health and being careful, your life expectancy is in bigger hands.

The other three variables do offer you a great deal of choice, and control, and offer you the opportunity to make more dramatic changes in order to build a plan that is both motivating and believable.

Let's look at each variable separately.

Future Income Needs

The first thing we need to do is by far the most important, and was the topic of discussion of the last chapter. That is, determine what your retirement will look like, and then *quantify* that in terms of an annual income.

This is precisely where most people get bogged down, or just skip over, and yet (as this entire book is dedicated to show you) this is the essence of creating a truly great future. Most people would prefer to just use the planner's "rule of thumb" and use 70% of their current income as the target income in retirement. This unfortunately misses the point entirely.

It may in fact turn out to be 70% of current income that you need, but more likely it's not. And without going through the exercise, you won't know. There will always be a doubt nagging at you. Furthermore, 70% of current income sounds like a cut in income, a step backwards, and that just doesn't sound very appealing. Aren't we supposed to look forward to retirement? Yes! Building an exciting, inspiring, motivating future is at the heart of retirement planning!

So how do we calculate our future income needs? Like writing an essay, the hardest part is getting started. Once you get going, your juices start to flow and the process takes on a life of its own. There are several ways you may approach this; here is perhaps the easiest way to get started.

> "Seize this very minute
> —Boldness has genius,
> power and magic in it.
> Only engage, and then
> the mind grows heated
> —Begin it, and then
> the work will be completed!"
> JOHANN WOLFGANG VON GOETHE

Start by preparing a list of the all the expenses you currently incur on a monthly and annual basis. On the same list, indicate what you expect, or plan, to spend on the same item in retirement. You should break the list into reasonable categories, such as the list below. A blank form similar to this one can be found in Appendix 1. You should go there now, and fill it in. Take your time. Gather the documents you may need to do this job properly, things like your chequebook, bank statements, credit card statements, and so on.

Expense Item	Current Annual Amount	Expected Amount in Retirement (today's dollars)
Mortgage	$20,000	Nil
Property taxes	$3,000	$3,000
Heat, hydro, water	$3,000	$3,000
Car:		
• monthly payments	$3,600	$3,600
• gas, maintenance	$2,400	$2,400
• insurance	$1,500	$1,500
Clothing and personal	$4,000	$4,000
Groceries	$8,600	$5,000
Dining out/entertainment	$2,000	$5,000
Children's expenses	$2,500	$1,000
Education savings (RESP)	$4,000	Nil
Healthcare	$1,000	$2,000
RRSP & Savings	$15,000	Nil
Travel and vacation	$3,000	$3,000
• "Golf dream" annual trip		$5,000
• Summer cottage rental		$3,000
Miscellaneous	$1,000	$1,000
TOTALS	**$74,600**	**$41,500**

What we have determined here is that we would like a net income (after tax) of $41,500 in retirement.

Notice, in this example, that the income needs in retirement are actually only 56% of current income needs! And that is after we *increase* travel and recreation expenses by $8,000 per year (to a total more than three times the current amount), *increase* the amount spent on dining and entertainment by $3,000, and *double* the amount on healthcare!

A word of caution. *This is only an example.* Your own worksheet should look a lot different, and the choices you make need to be right for you. No financial planner can tell you what to *want.* But if you know what you want, they can help you put the numbers down.

In particular, it's important to note that not everyone's planned retirement expenses work out to be lower than their current expenses. In fact, it's quite possible that you will want *considerably more* in retirement. That's perfectly acceptable.

For example, you may decide you want own a cottage and perhaps a condo in some warm climate. Both of these things will add considerably to your annual overhead. It would be quite easy to take the example above, and add new expenses so that retirement income needs exceed $100,000. Is that achievable? Anything is, if you believe it. And a plan will help to show you how.

So, if you find yourself reviewing my example and saying things like "He's way off with his assumption on healthcare," or thinking "Wow, I guess I don't need 70% of my current income in retirement," then you are on a dangerously wrong track. Stop looking at my example, and start constructing your own summary. There's no power for you in someone else's dream. The power is in your own.

Before we proceed, we should determine how much income we expect to receive from sources other than our investments: sources like government pensions, company pensions or some other form of income, such as rental properties. Subtract this amount, and we have the income required from our investments. If for example we expect to receive $10,000 per year (in current dollars) from a company pension plan, then we simply need to build a plan to realize the difference—$31,500 per year, using our example—through our investment income. Let's keep this example simple and assume that there will be *no* other sources of income.

This is an exercise you will want to spend some time on, and probably review every year. Look at your life as a work under construction. This chart represents your blueprints. Keep them handy, and review them often. Change them as necessary to keep your future unfolding in the direction of your dreams. Change is also the underlying theme of our next factor, inflation.

Inflation

Maybe $41,500 is the right number for today, but unless you're retiring today, it's not exactly the number we will use. We must project this income figure into the future, and that means we have to make an assumption with respect to inflation. It costs 46 cents to mail a first class letter today. Twenty years ago it was 6 cents. That's inflation.

What we need to remember when considering our assumption with respect to inflation (and rate of return) is that we are projecting over a long period of time. Even if you are relatively close to retirement now, you probably expect to be retired for a long time. You may expect the price of a stamp to stay the same over the next few years, but what about over the next 20, 30 or 40 years?

While you get to choose a number to use as an inflation assumption, you don't have any control over what the rate of inflation ultimately becomes. You need to choose an assumption that makes sense to you—a number that won't cause you to lose faith in your plan because you see it as too optimistic. Conversely, if you are too pessimistic, you may make your plan unnecessarily difficult!

This book isn't about economics, so let's not get bogged down by trying to pick the "right" inflation assumption. I think this is pretty simple. The most reasonable long-term assumption with respect to inflation in Canada is 3% or something very close to 3%. Why? The average rate of inflation in Canada from 1924 to 1997 was 3.1%.

Once you settle on this assumption, you shouldn't go back to change this number in an effort to revise your financial plan unless you become convinced for whatever reason that your initial assumption was not reasonable. That is to say, this doesn't become a pivot point to make your plan work out. It becomes fixed.

It's important to point out, when we assume that inflation will average 3%, what we are saying is that the cost of everything will increase by a compound rate of 3% each and every year. Of course, the average is just that, an average. Some years inflation will be much higher, and some years inflation will be much lower.

But if, for example, inflation was 3% over the next year, then the $41,500 we want in retirement income would grow to $42,757 over that one-year period (3% of $41,500 is $1,257, and $41,500 + $1,257 = $42,757). But retirement is probably more than one year away.

Time to Retirement

Before our inflation assumption can be applied, we need to know how many years there are between now and the date you want to retire.

Many people think that this isn't so much a variable as it is the *result* of all the other variables. I've had many clients ask me after I have gathered all the pertinent facts, "So tell us, *when* can we retire?" This perception is indeed unfortunate as it reduces retirement planning to an exercise in determining "how bad it's going to be."

It reinforces the mistaken belief that our dreams are out of reach. Your dreams *are* within reach. And you can retire when you want to.

Let's suppose for our example that you want to retire in 20 years. We need to extrapolate our inflation assumption over 20 years, instead of just one. How do you calculate the future value of $41,500 in 20 years without doing 20 separate calculations? (You *can* do 20 separate calculations if that works for you.) If you have a financial calculator, simply ask it to return the future value over 20 terms at 3% with a present value of $41,500. You will find the answer to be $74,954. Or, on a regular calculator you can calculate $41,500^* (1+.03)^{20}$. (Follow these steps. Enter 1.03. Now hit the button marked y^x. Now enter 20. Press the multiplication button (x) and enter 41500. Hit the equals button (=). The answer should be on the screen.) Or you can use a variety of software packages. Or you can ask your financial advisor. Choices abound.

The important thing is that we now know our income target for retirement. We need a spendable income of $74,954, in twenty years time.

Income Tax Rate

Of course, we all know that spendable income is much less than actual income. And we all know the reason—income taxes. When it comes to income tax I would suggest that we have little choice, and even less control.

The only reasonable assumption is to assume that when you retire, the tax rates will be roughly the same as they are today. The only reason *not* to assume this is because you believe that the government will make changes. Don't make assumptions based purely on some external event that is out of your control. That's a good way to add stress instead of relieve stress.

Yes, it may be logical to assume that the government will adjust the graduated tax table to account for inflation. The only problem with this assumption is that the track record to date suggests it's not true. Conversely, you may believe that things are going to get worse, and want to predict a tax rate higher than currently exists. How much worse can they get? If you suffer from this much pessimism, financial planning is going to be extremely difficult.

My advice is simple and logical. Stick with the current tax tables. Nothing needs to change in order for this to be an accurate assumption.

Let's further assume that you are married (or plan to be!) so what we are really trying to do is earn two incomes of $37,477 each ($74,954 ÷ 2). The question then is what income is needed to produce an after-tax income of $37,477? (Getting your retirement income neatly split into two may or may not involve some tax planning. This book is not about tax strategies, but good books on this subject are readily available. I suggest Tim Cestnick's book *Winning the Tax Game* as a good place to start.)

The answer can be found in your tax guide, from your accountant, or from a financial planner. But you will find that the average tax rate (in this example) is about 25%, and therefore a gross income of $49,969 will produce the required net income of $37,477 (37,477 ÷ 0.25 = 49,969). This represents half of our target, meaning that our gross income target is $99,939.

We're getting closer.

So what we need then, is investment income of $99,939 per year, starting 20 years from now, and increasing with inflation each year thereafter. The next question is, for how long?

Life Expectancy

Computer software will require you to provide the date you expect to die. Tough question, isn't it? If you have many years before retirement, it's easy to say something like 90 or 95 and feel pretty "safe" that you won't make it that far. Ask someone who's 75, or 85, or hey, 95!, and it's a different story.

It is not my intention to scare you into projecting a ridiculously long retirement requiring vastly increased sums of money to support. It *is* my intention to help you make your future as bright, secure, and exciting as possible. The truth is, you will die. Furthermore, your income needs may decline as you get older, or at least shift from one kind of expense to another. You likely won't be doing as much snorkeling when you're 90 as you did when you were 65. But here's my suggestion. First, assume that your income needs will continue to increase every year at the rate of inflation. Second, assume you will live forever.

The established theory is that as you get older you will dip into your capital, slowly using it up. If the plan works perfectly you would spend your last dollar on the day you died. That's the theory. In practice, most retirees don't *want* to dip into capital—either because they worry they may outlive the projections, or because they've already mentally given the money to their children. Consequently, most retirees *don't* dip into capital. They simply reduce their expenses to be in line with their income—and often it's declining.

In anticipation of perhaps feeling the same way, why not just build a plan that assumes you will live forever? That's the first reason I make this suggestion. The second reason is this: it will probably make much less difference to your plan than you think.

Let's look at our final factor and then revisit this.

Rate of Return on Investments

Among the six variables, rate of return is perhaps the most controversial, and it certainly gets the most attention. It is true that we have a great deal of choice here, and a great deal of control. For many, it *is* the key to the castle. We believe that if we can only earn enough on our investments, we will have no worries in retirement. Convinced it is of extreme importance, we scour the planet for the best investments, "best" being defined as those with the best return (and no risk, of course).

I won't regress into a long examination of investments and returns, but suffice it to say, this isn't as important as you might think. Once again, it's important to note that we are looking at a long time horizon. Even if you are retiring today, chances are you are projecting to live for 20 years, 30 years, or even longer. If you have 20 years to retirement, then the total time horizon might be 50 years!

The investment returns over one or two years can vary dramatically. Over 50 year periods, the variation between assets in the same group is barely noticeable (those groups being equities, fixed income, and cash). The issue is not which investment within the group, but rather, how much of your investment portfolio you allocate to that group. Your choice of asset group will ultimately determine a large percentage of your return. Yes, this is asset allocation.

This is an extremely important area of discussion for you and your financial advisor, or investment advisor. It's obviously not just a matter of picking the highest returning asset group, or even of dividing your assets evenly across all of the groups, thus "diversifying." It's about fitting your investment strategy into your overall financial plan, while giving due consideration to your "money personality" and your desire for a stress-free financial life. It's a big subject (and a good subject for another book!).

Let's just pick a number for this exercise. Since I'm writing the book, I'm going to pick 8%. Let's assume that *during retirement*, we will earn an average rate of 8% on our investments, indefinitely.

(Our investment returns leading *up* to retirement are, interestingly enough, not a factor in setting our retirement goal. They do become important when we start to calculate how much you need to save in order to reach it! More in the next chapter.)

Yes, I realize that choosing 8% (or whatever I might have chosen) should stir up a debate because it will seem too high, or too low. This is a question that relates to your investment strategy and can vary dramatically. Most experts will tell you that your assumptions should fall somewhere between 3% and 10%, depending on your investment choices. I'm choosing 8%. Based on my experience this is fairly conservative, using a balanced portfolio, relative to our 3% inflation assumption.

Please, don't get hung up on my number. It is *critical* that you choose your own assumption for rate of return, that you are comfortable with your number, and that when the time comes you invest in a way that renders your assumption possible.

Unfortunately, before we proceed we have to contend, once again, with inflation. We've accounted for inflation up to retirement, but we also need to account for it *during* retirement. In that sense, we want our pot of money to grow every year by 3% (our inflation assumption) so that what we earn from it will grow as well. If we have a return of 8% every year, 3% is needed to adjust for inflation. That leaves 5% for us! (The actual "inflation adjusted return" is a more complex calculation, but using this simple subtraction method produces a more conservative estimate—in other words, we'll surpass our estimates if we use this method. Besides, it's easier to understand.)

Get the calculator again. Now we need to determine how much money is required to generate $99,939 if the return is 5%. That's simply $99,939 divided by 5% which equals $1,998,780 ($99,939 ÷ .05 = $1,998,780). Let's round this up to $2 million.

There you have it. We start with a vision of what you want to be, do, and have in your retirement years. We end up with a goal. Based on our example, we need to accumulate $2 million. Two million dollars will generate a gross income of $99,939 every year, increasing at 3% each year, forever. In the forever sense, this number represents our "over the top" target.

Let's revisit the "life expectancy" assumption now that we have all the inputs gathered. Using Naviplan™, a financial planning software package from EISI of Winnipeg, we can recalculate our goal based on exhausting our funds at various ages (our life expectancy) as opposed to our obviously optimistic assumption of living forever.

Let's assume for the example that we are currently age 40, so our retirement age 20 years from now is age 60. (This is important, as we need to know how many years our funds must last. Obviously we'll need less money if retirement starts at age 65, and more money if retirement starts at age 55.)

Here are the results, rounded to the nearest tenth of a million ($100,000).

Life Expectancy (years)	85	90	95	100	Eternity
Target Amount (millions of dollars)	$1.5	$1.6	$1.7	$1.8	$2.0

So the issue ultimately boils down to either determining when you plan to expire (and conveniently run out of money at the same time) or, instead, planning to die incredibly rich.

The point is, if the eternity plan is within reach, why not go for it? It certainly *feels* a whole lot better! One reason might be that you are not comfortable leaving someone else a *great deal* of money (my address is elsewhere in this book). Other books and speakers will tell you that you should plan on dying broke. That's the same kind of negative thinking that would suggest you minimize your personal income so that you can maximize your share of government benefits. "I hope to be dependent on the government," and "I don't want to leave anything to anyone"—these don't sound like mottos for a fulfilling life. Freedom, independence, charity, and love sound a whole lot better.

> "No pessimist ever discovered the secrets of the stars or sailed to an uncharted land, or opened a new heaven to the human spirit."
>
> HELEN KELLER

As you develop a plan to accumulate this money, you will most likely make some changes affecting the ultimate amount. There are plenty of ways to adjust this. I think of it as a retirement goal machine. You put in the desired income, the rate of inflation, the years to retirement, the tax rate, life expectancy, and the rate of return, and you get a number that serves as a target. If you adjust any of these inputs, your target changes. If for example you change the rate of return to 9%, and leave everything else the same, the goal drops to $1.7 million. As you build the plan, simply turn the dials so that everything lines up.

One word of advice. Don't dial back your dream. Dial up your expectations.

Yes, there is some math involved in getting your retirement nailed down and, admittedly, the calculations made here are greatly simplified. There are, however, fantastic planning tools available today that make these calculations for you. You simply provide the assumptions. But just like your car, if you understand a little bit about how it's working, it's easier to know when things look right and wrong. Most importantly where this exercise is concerned, the more comfort you have with the process, the more likely you are to believe that it's a true reflection of *your* dreams. That's really what it is all about.

By now you should have a retirement goal—a number (probably a big one) that represents how much money you are going to accumulate before you retire. Take that number, write it down and pin it up where you will see it often. Better still, make a thermometer like the ones they use for hospital fundraisers and put your goal at the top. In our example, the top of the thermometer will say $2 million, 20 years from today. Around your thermometer hang pictures representative of your retirement—vacation destinations, golf courses, whatever is important to you. On the thermometer, fill in how much money you have to date.

> *"Don't bunt.*
> *Aim out of the ballpark.*
> *Aim for the company of immortals."*
> DAVID OGILVY

Now let's make a plan to accumulate the rest.

SUMMARY OF KEY POINTS

There are six factors, or variables, used in calculating how much money you will need to accumulate in order to realize your retirement dream:

1. Future income needs
2. Inflation
3. Years until retirement
4. Income tax rate
5. Life expectancy
6. Rate of return on investments

While you have choice over the assumptions you make with respect to all of these, your greatest choice lies with those over which you have the most control, namely, future income needs, years until retirement, and rate of return on investments.

Together these variables form a "retirement goal machine." As you adjust these assumptions, you produce different results. The exercise of setting a retirement goal is simply turning these dials until everything lines up.

The Retirement Goal Machine

_____
_____
_____
_____
_____
_____
_____
_____
_____
_____
_____
_____
_____
_____

_____
_____
_____
_____
_____

> *"I never did anything by accident,
> nor did any of my inventions come
> indirectly through accident..."*
> THOMAS A. EDISON

ACTION STEPS

Complete the cash flow chart in Appendix I. Focus on determining what your income needs are likely going to be in retirement. How do they differ from today?

Using this information and the steps in the book, can you estimate how much you need to accumulate in order to realize this retirement dream? Keep at this (get help if necessary) until you can.

5

WHAT IS
A FINANCIAL PLAN?

*"When schemes are laid in advance, it is surprising
how often the circumstances will fit in with them."*
WILLIAM OSLER

NOT so long ago there were three distinct pillars in the financial
services industry—banking, insurance, and securities. Today,
the distinction between these groups has been reduced to a blur, if
it hasn't altogether disappeared. What's even more interesting is
that all of them appear to be eagerly moving into a fourth arena—
financial planning.

Representatives and employees from all sectors of financial
services are increasingly using labels like Financial Advisor, or
Financial Consultant, or Financial Planner to describe who they
are. This has regulators more than a little concerned.

Convinced that *salespeople* are using these labels to lure customers
into purchasing their products—be that insurance, mutual funds,
or other investments—the regulators are anxious to put restrictions
on the use of such titles. (More on this in the next chapter.) For
now, suffice it to say that a great deal of attention is being devoted
to the question "Who really *is* a financial planner?"

There seems to be an obvious definition. A financial planner is
one who prepares financial plans. Since this is simple to the sublime,

it will never suffice as the "acid test" in the eyes of the regulators. (If these same regulators were providing labels to the animal kingdom, squirrels would need to pass a multiple choice exam on trees and nuts before being allowed to call themselves squirrels.)

Nonetheless, my definition begs another question. What is a financial plan? Here's where it gets dicey.

Ask a fee-for-service financial planner and most likely he will reach into his desk drawer and pull out a sample financial plan. This plan will be luxuriously bound and contain somewhere in the neighbourhood of 50 or more pages. It will provide great detail about the subject's current financial picture accompanied by the appropriate charts and graphs, and then detail one or more long-term strategies to accomplish one or more financial goals. It will probably deal with cash flow, estate objectives, retirement goals, tax planning, and perhaps education funding. It will look so wonderfully professional that you will immediately be convinced that it must contain a wealth of important information. Information that will unlock the secret door of wealth.

> "An intelligent plan is the first step to success. The man who plans knows where he is going, knows what progress he is making and has a pretty good idea when he will arrive."
>
> BASIL S. WALSH

Ask a top mutual fund salesperson and you may get a completely different answer. He may start asking you some important questions about where you are now, and where you want to go, and jot down bits of relevant information on a napkin he grabs from the table. Then he will punch some of those numbers into his financial calculator with such speed that you will wonder if he's just pretending, like some actor in a play. Then with the confidence of a CEO he will spin the napkin around to face you and tell you *exactly* what you need to do, in simple steps, to get what you want. His conviction, enthusiasm, and confidence will leave you convinced he's right.

The truth is both of these may well be the right response to the question. Both could be valid financial plans. And this is a chilling reality to both the fee-for-service financial planner, *and* the fund salesperson, who considers himself a commission-based financial planner.

The fee-for-service professional wonders, "How can this sales person scribble a few things on a napkin, and dare to call this a financial plan?" His real fear, of course, is that his fee is being called into question. He charges a fee based on the fact that he spends many hours working on the detailed financial plan. Yet this upstart salesperson is spending only a few minutes to come up with his recommendations, and is charging no fee!

On the other hand, the mutual fund salesperson wonders, "How can this fee-for-service planner charge this huge fee for something of so little benefit?" His real fear, of course, is that he doesn't want to take the time, or deal with the training involved, in constructing these often complex financial plans. Furthermore, he sees no benefit in doing them. And he worries that regulators may force him to change the way he does business.

> *"Each man should frame life so that at some future hour fact and his dreamings meet."*
> VICTOR HUGO

So how do you choose what's right for you? At which extreme, or where on the continuum if these represent the extremes, can you find a financial plan that will get the job done for you?

A friend of mine says, "If you want a better answer, ask a better question." In the previous paragraph lies the seed of a better question. *What should a financial plan do for you?*

The important thing is not what a financial plan *is*, but rather what a financial plan *does for us*. It's not how many pages, but how effective it is that counts. Let's look at a financial plan from this perspective. I think you will see what I mean.

What should a financial plan do for you? In answering that question, there are six key points:

1. Set/clarify your goals.
2. Determine your present situation.
3. Map the route(s) to your goals.
4. Build belief.
5. Keep it simple.
6. Motivate and inspire.

Let's look at each one.

Set/Clarify Your Goals

This was the subject of the last chapter, and is a rather obvious aspect of any plan. An interesting question, however, is this: Which comes first, the plan or the goal?

Keep in mind that a goal must be specific and measurable. In the last chapter we arrived at a specific and measurable goal with respect to retirement—*how much money* and *how soon* being the parameters. This goal didn't come from a financial plan. It came from a vision.

The problem with a goal that comes directly from a vision is that we often find it difficult to believe. We have no action plan to realize it, so it just sits there in the form of a wish. Your local lottery corporation uses the slogan "imagine the freedom" in their advertising. This very effectively gets your visioning process, your imagination, to go to work and you paint a picture of what your world could be like if only you won the big one. Then presumably you buy the lottery ticket. Really though, your confidence in the realization of this dream is pretty dismal. Not too many people (hopefully) rush out and buy a dream house based on the purchase of a lottery ticket.

In truth then, while our vision gives rise to some important goals, those goals lack substance without something else—without a plan to realize them. Furthermore, a plan will help to refine the goals. The initial goals act as a benchmark. The financial plan makes the goal specific.

For example, from our efforts in Chapter 4 we determined that in order to retire in 20 years with a net after-tax income of $41,500 we must accumulate $2 million. We made specific assumptions with respect to taxation, investment return, life expectancy and inflation. In some instances we took the simplest route in order to keep things understandable. During the financial planning process we will tighten those assumptions and perhaps use different values at different stages. We may also want to make more exact tax calculations based on who earns the income and what type of income it is.

These and a variety of other changes that we may entertain will most likely cause our final goal to change. Given that we generally took the most conservative route in our first attempt, we ended up with a conservative target. As your plan takes shape, your goal will appear easier to reach.

The first step involved in retirement planning is to create the vision. Ask the question, "What do I really want?" and let the answer to that question be your guide. Then, through the process of building a financial plan to realize that dream, you will come up with some specific, measurable goals. One of these goals will be a sum of money at a specific time—your retirement goal.

The process then becomes:

CREATE		CONSTRUCT		DETERMINE
THE	→	A	→	THE
VISION		FINANCIAL PLAN		GOALS

Far too often we see this as being exactly the other way around. We come up with goals—goals like "I want 70% of my current income in retirement." Then we build a plan to realize this goal. Then we imagine what our life can be like based on this income level. This is survival mode. Hanging on. It's based on fear. And it's less than inspiring.

> *"Make sure you visualize what you really want, not what someone else wants for you."*
> JERRY GILLIES

When you *start* with the vision, you can operate without the shackles of money. You can, to borrow from the lottery, "imagine the possible." This is not easy to do, but it is immensely rewarding.

Then, you start to contemplate *how*. Sometimes, the how will seem so difficult that the vision will fade. It will seem impossible and so you will surrender to the shackles of reality. Again, that's unfortunate. There is always a way. If you can imagine it, it can be. Keep looking for the path.

> *"If we did the things we are capable of doing, we would literally astound ourselves."*
> THOMAS A. EDISON

Eventually we see that in truth this process is not linear, but rather it is circular. Visioning gives rise to planning. Planning helps to define goals. But both can and will influence each other, and influence the vision!

We can hop on this circle at any point. Most of us start with goals and make the plan and the vision fit into those goals. This of course guarantees that instead of getting what we want, we get what we believe we deserve, or what we believe is possible given our perceived limitations. The key to self-fulfillment, to getting what we want, and what we truly deserve, is to focus our attention on the vision. The ultimate in self-fulfillment is to give the vision 100% weighting—to make our plans and goals line up with our ultimate vision.

At the end of this exercise of fine-tuning your plan and your vision, goals will be created. These goals must be specific and measurable. They must be your own. They must be inspiring. And you must believe they are achievable (even just barely achievable is okay). If they aren't, keep going. Your planning isn't done yet.

An important thing to know about goals comes from a book by James Mapes. In *Quantum Leap Thinking* he says, "Goals are absolutely necessary and absolutely limiting." The secret to this visioning → planning → goal-setting process is found in this simple truth. As has been well discussed in this book, goals are absolutely essential. They provide us with a target and focus our energies on achieving our heart's desires. They work. But they also provide us with boundaries.

When we hit a goal we initially feel the satisfaction of accomplishment, but generally we also wonder "What if I had set the goal higher?" Standing at age 65 with a $2 million investment portfolio may bring great satisfaction—especially if you set out to do just that. But you may also wonder—"What if I had set my goal at $4 million? Or $10 million?"

This kind of thinking may lead to the conclusion that you should avoid setting goals, and simply "go for the most you can get." This of course is a slippery slope that leads to a high stress life. Instead of focussing on the accomplishment of specific goals, you end up on the eternal treadmill, on a race with no finish line. You spend your life looking for higher returns, and lower costs. You avoid all help offered to you—help costs money—and you move in and out of risky investments, usually at the wrong times, in order to outsmart the market. Ultimately, you end up with less.

Goals are absolutely necessary. But they will change. You will continually find yourself on the circle of visioning, planning and goal setting. As your life expands you need to revisit your vision and continually ask yourself *Am I reaching for all that I truly want?* If the answer is yes, be at peace. If the answer is no, revisit the plan, and get back on the circle. Your goals will need to change.

The important thing is this. When you have finished (for now) your financial plan you need to have some clearly defined goals. They are *essential*.

Determine Your Present Situation

It seems rather obvious, but before you set out on any journey, you must first find your own location on the map. This is deceptively simple.

This isn't just a matter of saying "You are here" and putting a big arrow on the map. This is really about getting organized. It's about seeing the big picture—for many it's seeing the big picture for the first time in a long time, maybe the first time ever.

Think about the last time your work life was completely disorganized. (Maybe now? My apologies, and admiration, to those who are never disorganized.) Your desk was a mess, with papers stacked in meaningless piles, and messages scattered about the desk on sticky notes and various other scraps of paper. Several projects you were working on were piled one on top of the other. You weren't sure whether or not you were working on the most important thing to do—it just happened to be on top of the pile and had your attention. As you worked, you started to wonder about all the important things that needed to be done that were currently hidden from view. Sounds stressful, doesn't it?

The solution here is painfully obvious. You need to get organized. You need to sort through everything on your desk and either file it or throw it out. Create a separate pile for reading and put it in a "to be read" pile somewhere other than on your desk. As you go, you need to create a list of things to do which will include projects, and phone calls to return.

When you are finished you will have one sheet of paper on your desk. That sheet of paper will be your list of things to do. Sort them in order of priority. Now put the sheet aside and start to work on number one. Feeling more relaxed?

If you have been through this experience you will know some of the important benefits. You are much less stressed, and you are much more effective.

The same is true of your financial life. In order to be relaxed and effective with your money you need to be organized. You need to create a summary of all of your assets and liabilities, a balance sheet or statement of net worth. (Appendix II contains a blank balance sheet.) And you need a step-by-step plan.

It's also important to accurately take stock of what you currently have for the journey. Outlining your current investments and liabilities will allow you to more accurately project where you are currently headed. If your financial plan is going to be valuable to you, it needs to start *exactly* where you are now.

Map the Route(s) to Your Goals

The question is, can you get there from here? We know where here is, and we know where there is. Can we join the two without having to cross any impassable mountains?

The important thing here is that a financial plan provide details about the entire route. Far too often we settle for less and make statements like "If I save $100 per month, every month, I should be fine." Yes, you are headed in the right direction. But you may not end up where you're hoping to end up—at least not when you were hoping to get there.

If you want to fly from Halifax to London you could just head east over the Atlantic Ocean. But that statement holds true if you want to fly to virtually every destination in the U.K., Europe, Asia and Africa. You need to be more specific.

Creating a complete map also helps to make sure that you are mapping the course over the true topography of your life. Let's return to the example of accumulating $2 million dollars in 20 years. If you choose an investment rate of 8% as your assets accumulate, and assume that you will invest the same amount every month for the next 20 years, the amount you need to save every month is $3,395 (starting from $0 today). That will most likely appear to be far too much initially, because it represents a straight-line approach.

When we construct the map over the realities of your life, it becomes much more reasonable, and achievable. First of all, we should assume that you will save an increasing amount each year as your income increases. So you will save less now, but more later. Next, we can assume that once your mortgage is paid off, you can direct a large chunk of that monthly commitment to your investments. There will likely be other areas of your life that will either provide an opportunity to save more, or require a greater amount of your cash flow. The best way to see these opportunities is to create a cash flow projection, which becomes part of your map.

A cash flow projection is simply a summary of how much you expect to spend, itemized to a reasonable degree, year by year over the entire planning period. This needn't be overly complicated. Most of our expense categories, such as groceries, entertainment, travel, and housing,

> *"Can you think of anything more permanently elating than to know that you are on the right road at last?"*
> VERNON HOWARD

remain relatively consistent over time, simply increasing with inflation. Others will change more dramatically, such as mortgages and children's education costs, and these offer us the most opportunity for planning.

Once all of these factors are taken into consideration, it is quite likely that your commitment today will need to be much less— closer to $1,000 per month as opposed to $3,000 per month!

This year-by-year map will also give you annual checkpoints, allowing you to make minor adjustments to stay on course.

Build Belief

If you really want to know the secret to all of this, it's this: Belief. We get what we believe we will get in life. Nothing less and nothing more. We can dream and set goals. We can pursue those goals and do all the right things, but if we don't have faith in what we are doing, at some point we will stop, and accept what we have been believing all along.

Perhaps the most important aspect of the financial planning process is that it helps build belief in your dreams. This is not well understood, even by most financial planners.

> *"The mind is the limit. As long as the mind can envision the fact that you can do something, you can do it—as long as you really believe 100 percent."*
> ARNOLD SCHWARZENEGGER

For some, building belief is remarkably easy. For these people, a few simple calculations will quickly show that they are virtually already there. Staying on course is all they need to do. Belief then is almost instantaneous. Now the question should be, is this all I really want, or can I create a better vision?

For others, the challenge of believing will remain a challenge. For these people the financial plan must be more graduated, with easier-to-achieve goals set for the first few years, and then more challenging goals as confidence builds. These people will also need to spend more time reworking their plans, and finding the right balance between the plan and their vision.

Remember, this is a dynamic process for everyone. It will change as your life changes. You should be encouraged to hang on to your initial vision even if your plan takes you somewhere that falls short. Here's the reason. As you move along the path dictated by your plan, you will discover ideas and opportunities that are presently hidden from view. These new ideas and opportunities will always point you to your true vision, or a better one, so long as you hang on to it. That's the power of belief.

A plan that leaves you doubtful is all but useless. In fact, it's worse, because it's discouraging. You need to be encouraged. You need to move forward with confidence. You need to believe.

Keep it Simple

Essentially, your plan needs to be understandable. Not understandable by a Ph.D. in Economics. Understandable by you.

Unless you speak Spanish, try putting together a gas barbecue using only the Spanish instructions (no peeking at the diagrams) and you will get a sense of what I am trying to point out. For one, it's hard, if not impossible, to believe.

There's a tendency in the world of money to believe that complex is better. This belief is largely driven by our desire to "bob and weave" around a very complex tax system. In far too many instances these strategies merely

> *"Life is really simple, but men insist on making it complicated."*
> CONFUCIUS

take us on a longer, more complicated road, to exactly the same place. In these cases, the real cost of saving a few tax dollars is increased stress and perhaps some sleepless nights.

Your financial plan should reduce stress, not increase it. Building a financial plan isn't just about creating a better future; it's also about creating a better now. Don't compromise—get both.

If your plan calls for some tax strategy or investment that you simply don't understand, change it. There is always another way, and the strategy you understand will always be the best for you.

Motivate and Inspire

Many financial planners will disagree on this point. They will maintain that it is not their job to *motivate* you to do anything. Their job, as they see it, is to show you the numbers—the hard facts, if you will—and let you do with them what you choose. This perhaps is the great dividing line between fee-for-service planners and commissioned salespeople. The commissioned sales person may tell you that all they do is provide motivation. If they can motivate you and get you moving in the *right* direction, even without a plan, at least you will be better off than you were when you were standing still!

As usual, both are wrong, and right. You need both. You need the facts and figures—this gets you organized, shows you what to do next, and helps you build the belief necessary to realize your dreams. But you also need to be motivated to take action. And it's important that the source of this motivation be positive. The most positive source of motivation is inspiration. We can be motivated to give our money away at gunpoint. That's not inspiring. We can be motivated to accumulate money by a grand vision of what our life can be like. That's inspiring.

> *"It's so hard when I have to.*
> *It's so easy when I want to."*
> SONDRA ANICE BARNES

In truth, if your financial plan scores ten out of ten on the first five points, it will motivate you—by inspiring you. This is the acid test. If you take your plan, review it and find yourself inspired, it must be right. If it doesn't inspire you, it still needs work.

This brings us back to the initial question—"What is a financial plan?" Well, if you have at least one specific goal, and starting from where you are, you know each and every step necessary to get to the goal, you believe it will be achieved, you understand all of the steps, and you find it inspiring enough to get you started and keep you going, then congratulations! You have a financial plan. The dream that started it is now your reality. Nothing can stop you.

This might have taken 50 pages and several hours of work, or it may have been scratched out on the back of a napkin over lunch. Does it really matter?

SUMMARY OF KEY POINTS

The important question is not *What is a financial plan* but *What should a financial plan do for me*. The answer to that question is contained in six key points:

1. Set/clarify your goals.
2. Determine your present situation.
3. Map the route(s) to your goals.
4. Build belief.
5. Keep it simple.
6. Motivate and inspire.

When your plan does all of these things, no matter how many pages it contains, it will enable you to reach for your dreams, and achieve your vision.

ACTION STEPS

Using the six key ingredients, construct your own financial plan. Before you begin, read Chapter 6. You may want to get the help of a good financial advisor.

_____
_____
_____
_____
_____
_____

> "Man's mind, once stretched
> by a new idea, never regains
> its original dimensions."
> OLIVER WENDELL HOLMES, JR.

_____
_____
_____
_____
_____
_____
_____
_____
_____
_____
_____
_____
_____
_____
_____
_____
_____
_____
_____
_____
_____
_____
_____
_____
_____
_____
_____
_____
_____

6

How to Find
a Financial Advisor

"There is no such thing as a self-made man.
You will reach your goals only with the help of others."
George Shinn

THE problem for me in telling you how to find a financial
advisor is that *I am* a financial advisor, and you might take
that into account as you read this. I will attempt not to be self-
serving.

This book is about financial planning and that may imply that
what you are looking for is a financial *planner*. However, to be
consistent with all of the recommendations I have made thus far,
and will make in the rest of this book, the person you should actually
be looking for is really an advisor, or coach, who is also a financial
planner.

The first assumption, already made, is that you do in fact want
help. There are some who are actually better off taking a do-it-
yourself approach. These people are definitely in the minority in
the same way that those who should repair their own brakes on
their car are in the minority. For those people, skip ahead. This
chapter will be of little value to you.

Many people *want* help, but are afraid to step into the minefield
of advisors to find one. Many others have an "advisor" but wonder

if they are getting what they want and need. Yet others wonder if they really want an advisor at all, and if so, what do they want an advisor to do? This chapter is for all of you.

> "Try not to become a man of success but rather try to become a man of value."
> ALBERT EINSTEIN

Most of the time when this subject is approached, it is from the perspective of knowledge and skills. The alphabet soup of designations lengthening the titles of everyone in financial services attests to our deep-rooted belief that knowledge is everything. Knowledge is certainly important. You probably don't want your dentist to rewire your house, or your electrician to pull your teeth. But in our zest to find the right qualifications we may overlook something even more important. Character.

Let's start by reviewing the last chapter. We have determined that a financial plan needs to do six things for us:

1. Set/clarify your goals.
2. Determine your present situation.
3. Map the route(s) to your goals.
4. Build belief.
5. Keep it simple.
6. Motivate and inspire.

Most financial planners will readily accept, and be able to sufficiently convince you, that they can help you accomplish points 2 and 3. They may disagree with the need to be involved in the others.

First of all, they may say, *your* goals are your business. You need to know what you want *before* you meet with an advisor, or they simply can't help you. Thanks for coming out. But as we noticed in the last chapter, while your goals originate from your personal vision, they take shape and are refined *during* and not before the planning process. Your financial planner should indeed play a significant role in shaping your goals.

With respect to building belief, many advisors will simply say that facts are facts. Chances are these are the same planners who will tell you that you *can't* have the life you want because you don't make enough money, or you're too conservative, or you spend too much. Avoid these people. Pessimism is contagious.

Keeping it simple really means making something understandable. Knowing something doesn't instantly make you a good communicator or teacher. Your plan will be useless if you don't understand it. Don't let someone impress you with how much they know. Be impressed when they show you how much *you* know.

> *"The authority of those who profess to teach is often a positive hindrance to those who desire to learn."*
> CICERO

Motivate and inspire? To many advisors, this just doesn't appear to belong in this discussion at all. To them, plans should help you see reality, not take you off into some fantasyland of excitement. Too bad for them. Life can be boring. We can spend our lives playing defense, holding on to what little we have (or perceive we have). We can spend our lives grounded in the reality of the here and now. But this is the hard way to live. Alternatively, we can stretch, and reach for more. We can live our lives growing and finding new ways to experience who we are. The choice is yours. Choose your advisors accordingly.

The advisor we should be looking for is much more than a competent technician (although she should also be that). The advisor we want must also be a good communicator, a confidant and counselor, a champion for our dreams, and an inspiration. Don't worry, these people are out there. Let's look at how you can find them.

I have discovered that most of the issues concerning "how to find a financial advisor" can be put into one of three categories:

> *"Coming together is a beginning;*
> *keeping together is progress;*
> *working together is success."*
> HENRY FORD

1. Relationship.
2. Skills and abilities.
3. Motivation.

Let's look at each.

Relationship

This is the issue that is most often overlooked. We don't think of having a relationship with our mechanic, appliance repairman, banker, or hair stylist, and so we assume that forging a relationship with a financial advisor is unnecessary as well. But I believe that the best way to understand what you are looking for, and to assess potential candidates, is to understand that you *are* looking for a relationship—probably a *long-term* relationship.

Consider Mary who has brought home Joe, a potential spouse, to meet her parents. During a quiet moment with Mom, she tells her the following: "Mom, Joe will make the perfect husband. He has a great career with regular hours at work and great pay. He is kind and gentle, funny and interesting. He is handsome. I know he'll make a good father. There's nothing about him you can find fault with. There's only one problem. I really don't love him."

What advice will Mom give her daughter? There's little doubt what Mom should say. "Dump him." The fact is, when you are looking to establish a relationship your priorities are different than when you are looking for someone to "do a job" for you. Most companies would be infinitely better served if they looked at future employees through the relationship lens first.

Obviously, finding a financial advisor is quite different from finding a spouse. You probably won't live with your financial advisor, and your commitment needn't be quite so serious. But it will be a relationship nonetheless.

In a relationship there is (or should be) mutual respect, trust, a willingness to listen and a desire to help. Look at these qualities again. Don't you want your financial advisor to possess these characteristics?

Many will still argue that it's not necessary for you to "like" your advisor. (It certainly *isn't* necessary that you *love* them!) If you have a competent advisor who's doing the right things for you, isn't it all right if you find her somehow *un*likable? Definitely not.

> *"When dealing with people, remember you are not dealing with creatures of logic, but with creatures of emotion."*
> DALE CARNEGIE

First of all, why settle for less? Don't compromise in life.

Secondly, and more importantly, if you don't like your advisor, how inspiring can that advisor be? How can you share your most important dreams, your ultimate vision, with someone you don't like? Quite simply, you won't.

Perhaps the key word in any relationship, but most certainly in your relationship with a financial advisor, is trust. There must be trust, or the purpose of the relationship—fulfillment of your financial dreams—is threatened. Trust—complete trust—is essential.

Trusting someone to do a competent job, to complete the job accurately and with your own best interests at heart, is where it starts. But that is only the beginning. You must also trust that your advisor will respect your values and your beliefs. You must trust that your advisor will respect your vision, or you simply cannot share it.

It is important to note that your relationship with a financial planner should not end when the plan is "complete." In fact, the plan is never complete, and that's the point. One reason I prefer the term "financial advisor" is that it implies, as it should, much more than simply construction of a plan. A plan is pointless without implementation. Who better to assist you with the implementation of a plan than the planner? Who better to assist you with the construction of a building than the architect?

Furthermore, your plan will need to change. It must change, almost by design! It may be only as we achieve the milestones laid out in our plan that we realize the power and potency of the goals we set out. This new-found understanding and belief empowers us to strive for more. The plan must change to reflect that.

Even apart from that, we all know that our lives are far from static. We change careers, add new family members, lose others. These and other changes in our lives affect our vision of the future. As our vision changes, so must our plan! So you see, financial planning isn't a one-time event.

So what we are looking for in a financial advisor is someone with whom we can have a long-term, win-win relationship. With that in mind, here are some questions to ask or issues to raise with potential advisors.

1. *Do I like this person?* The answer will require that you spend some time getting to know the advisor. Don't be afraid to ask personal questions, about family, hobbies, and so on—things that are important to you. No, you aren't trying to get invited over for dinner, or out for a round of golf (although either or both may happen) but you learn a lot more about someone's

character by learning about what they do off the job. It is also important to note that this will take time. Don't rush things. Look for an advisor who isn't rushing you. There's no hurry. If the advisor seems in a rush, you should wonder why.

2. *Do I trust this person?* *Trust* will most definitely follow *like*. It's hard to like someone you don't trust and vice-versa. But trust can be almost instantaneous—kind of a gut feeling. If you initially find yourself trusting the advisor, that's good, but move slowly. If you find yourself initially not trusting the advisor, chances are you never will. Keep looking.

3. *Will I be proud to introduce this person to my friends and family?* In case this appears to be a pitch to give your advisor referrals, it isn't. And frankly, if someone is asking you for the names of your friends and family too early in your relationship, I wonder how much of a relationship will ever really exist. But here's a great test for you to try. Imagine you are at a party and this potential advisor shows up. All your friends and family are there. It would appear that your advisor knows none of them (the advisor is there with a friend of a friend). The question is not *would* you introduce the advisor to your friends and family, but how would you *feel* in doing so? If it's a little uncomfortable, beware. If you are delighted to see the advisor, and eagerly speak about how happy you are to have found him, then things are looking good. Relationships are based on emotions. Check yours at every opportunity.

4. *Do our values and beliefs line up reasonably well?* Even happily married couples won't have identical values and beliefs. But they won't likely have any major conflicts either. If your advisor

tends to have a negative outlook and you are (or want to be) an optimist, you will likely find it hard to build a relationship. Once again, to get at this issue, you will most likely need to find out about the advisor's personal life (something I strongly recommend). You should also ask to read their business vision and mission statements, and have them provide examples of how they live those words. People generally are what they believe. Find out what that is.

Skills and Abilities

You might have a great relationship with your neighbour, but unless he has the skills and abilities to be your financial advisor, I recommend you find someone else.

This is an area of great focus among regulators and critics of the financial services industry. It almost always, however, ends up in a debate over specific designations. We have become completely enchanted with the little letters behind someone's name. It's a dangerous thing.

> *"Wise men don't need advice.*
> *Fools won't take it."*
> BENJAMIN FRANKLIN

Getting one's Certified Financial Planner (CFP) designation, for example, may mean that one is in fact a competent financial planner, or it may mean that one is good at studying and writing exams, and furthermore is motivated to have the right credentials. I'm not trying to make you suspicious, just cautious. I think the skills-and-abilities issue needs to be considered from a perspective other than an examination of credentials. Let's discuss how we might do that.

Every financial advisor you meet will have some skills and abilities based on their training, their level of knowledge, and their experience. What you want to find out is whether or not the skills and abilities they have match what you are looking for. So what are you looking for?

Once again, it is important to note that your relationship with your advisor will span many different aspects of your financial life. The beginning will be creating a plan. This will involve assessing where you are now, creating a vision for your future, and constructing a plan to get from here to there. So step number one is determining whether or not the potential advisor can do this, and whether or not they are in fact doing it.

Once the plan is complete, you also want your advisor to assist you in its implementation. The possibilities here are quite diverse.

Quite likely your plan will call for some investment management. So a financial advisor skilled in the area of investments will be important. That doesn't mean someone who buys and sells stocks. In fact, most people who buy and sell stocks call themselves "money managers," "stock brokers," or "investment advisors," and they will tell you that this is a full-time job. It's unlikely that they will have the time (or competency) to also construct a plan or deal with the other issues that we will discuss. Your financial advisor should be able to build an investment portfolio in which the active management of your portfolio is passed on to appropriate parties, be that mutual fund managers, wrap accounts, investment advisors, or someone similar. The important thing is that your advisor demonstrates ability and confidence in assisting you with this component.

Your plan may also call for life insurance or disability insurance, or both. All financial plans should touch on estate planning, but you will find that your interest in this subject—and your tendency to put estate planning as a priority—increases as you get older. So life insurance will at different times in your life and to different degrees, play an important role.

It's easy to find the lowest rates. It's quite another thing to find the most appropriate contracts, the best companies to deal with, and the right balance between paying insurance premiums and investing your dollars. Only an advisor competent in both investment management and insurance can do the latter.

Here's a great question to ask a potential advisor. Where does your revenue come from—in percentages? If an advisor earns 95% of revenue from investments and 5% from insurance, then you may question the competency in the area of insurance.

Your plan may also call for tax strategies outside the usual. It is quite likely that you should use the services of a competent accountant and lawyer as well as a financial advisor. Once again, these people will tell you that keeping up with current tax law is a full-time job. They don't have time to become financial planners, and neither do financial advisors have time to keep up with current tax laws. So the issue here becomes the extended network of your advisor, or perhaps their compatibility with your present accountant or lawyer. You should ask a potential advisor where he gets assistance in the area of taxation. Beware of the advisor who says, "I do it myself." You might also ask them to meet with your accountant, and let your accountant ask some questions. During that meeting, try to assess how comfortable the advisor feels meeting with the accountant.

You may also have priorities that touch on other areas. Education funding and the new RESP rules, for example. Or maybe you have just inherited a bond portfolio and need some advice on that. If you go to an advisor with no expertise in bonds, don't be surprised if he recommends you sell them all and invest elsewhere. Or perhaps you want to build a succession plan for your business and are looking for an advisor with experience in that area. Whatever skills you think you need, or may need, should be assessed in any advisor you meet with.

As you can see, there are a great number of potential areas to deal with. Few advisors today possess all of the skills necessary to provide you with "one stop shopping." But if you deal with a number of advisors in different areas, you will likely find them playing tug of war for your dollars. The ideal is to find an advisor who can help you prioritize, and most effectively integrate those priorities. This person may be a true generalist, or she may be a "quarterback" and work as part of a team. More and more financial services organizations are recognizing the importance of this, and they are adding competent professionals in areas not previously handled by their firm. If you are going to be working with a team, it is probably wise to meet the various players of that team before your proceed.

Motivation

(Hopefully it won't be too obvious already, but it should be noted that I have a bias toward commission-based planners, as I am one myself. I place a great value on long-term relationships and find it works best when I don't charge a fee. But let me say emphatically, there are excellent fee-for-service planners and excellent commission-based planners. You should judge neither on the basis of how they get compensated. Determine what's important to you and find the advisor that fits that description. This is not a one-size-fits-all area.)

One of the great debates going on in the financial planning world (a debate that has been going on for some time) is the debate over the pros and cons of the fee-for-service financial planner versus the commission-based financial planner. Although this debate always centres on compensation, what it really boils down to is the issue of motivation.

> *"No man,
> for any considerable period,
> can wear one face to himself,
> and another to the multitude,
> without finally getting bewildered
> as to which may be the true."*
> NATHANIEL HAWTHORNE

So that we are all on the same page, let's quickly review the differences between these two types of planners.

A fee-for-service financial planner charges a flat fee to produce a specific financial plan. In a sense, you are paying them for their time. If you want a basic retirement plan the fee be may relatively low. If you want a plan that encompasses not only retirement, but also cash flow, risk management, estate planning, tax planning, and education funding, the fee is likely to be much higher. Generally you will receive a letter of engagement at the outset which will tell you what they are going to do for you, and how much you are going to pay.

A commission-based financial planner charges no up-front fee but instead is compensated by commissions earned on financial products which you purchase through them. Investment funds, securities, life insurance, and disability insurance, to name a few, all generate (or at least can generate) commissions paid out at the time the transaction is made or contract put into effect. Some of these are negotiable, and some are not. Most of these products also generate ongoing commissions called renewals, or trailer fees, paid out over a number of years, sometimes as long as the product remains "in force." Because they are compensated by the supplier company through these commissions, a commission-based financial planner is not likely to charge you any fee to produce a financial plan.

Most, if not all, financial services professionals are at least partially motivated by money. Let's face it, all businesses are established to make a profit, and a financial services organization is a business.

But the fee-for-service versus commission debate focuses on the impact of the money motivation present in the relationship. Both sides like to accuse the other of manipulating the client to make a buck.

The argument goes like this:

Pro fee-for-service financial planner

If you are in the fee-for-service camp, you contend that a commission-based planner is in truth a salesperson. The sole motivation for doing a financial plan is to get you to buy something, which in turn generates a commission. Furthermore, if you are really skeptical, you suspect that these charlatans in fact sell only a limited number of products, usually from one company. This being the case, the financial plan is going to be distorted in order to point out the need for the particular product or products which they want you to buy. Once the plan is done (if in fact one is done at all) they will pester you into buying something in an effort to get paid.

On the other hand, the fee-for-service planner is completely objective and without bias. They won't steer you into any product or service, and they won't pester you after the plan is done. Their job is simply to provide you with an accurate and thorough outline of where you are now, where you want to go, and the potential routes to get there. Their competency in the area of financial planning is unquestionable. That is all they do.

Pro commission-based financial planner

Let's look at this now from the point of view of the commission-based planner. They contend that the fee-based planner is merely a technician. They don't disagree that fee-for-service financial planners are competent. But they do question the value of a plan that sits on a shelf collecting dust, which is where it will be without the guidance and motivation provided by someone who wants you to take the action necessary to get what you want. Furthermore, without the commission from financial products, fee-based planners have to charge fairly hefty fees in order to make a decent living. If you proceed to implement the strategies suggested, which you should, you will turn around and pay a commission (indirectly) to someone else! You are paying twice for the same advice! Furthermore, what kind of relationship will exist with a fee-for-service planner? Isn't it a one-time event? Kind of a one-night stand?

On the other hand, commission-based planners provide you with something most of us believe is too good to be true—something for nothing. They will assist you in building a financial plan, and charge you no fee. Many will argue that they are every bit as competent as the fee-for-service planners that charge an arm and a leg (metaphorically speaking). Then they will stick around, and in fact be highly motivated, to help you put your plan into action. And if things go well, and they should, they will act as your financial advisor on an ongoing basis. A relationship of trust and respect develops and you have a financial "coach" for life. All of this costing you nothing.

Both sides have great arguments. Neither is entirely right, or wrong.

> "It is the individual who is not interested in his fellow men who has the greatest difficulties in life and provides the greatest injury to others. It is from among such individuals that all human failures spring."
> ALFRED ADLER

Ultimately, both sides have the same motivation. Money. The fee-for-service planner wants to convince you that the commission-based planner is dangerous. If they succeed you use their services and they make money. The commission-based planner wants to convince you that you are wasting your money on a fee-for-service plan. If they succeed, you use their services, and probably, they make money.

The truth is, if the *focus* is on how they make their profit, *both* kinds of planners are equally dangerous. It's quite simple if you remember that you are trying to build a relationship. Can you have a solid relationship with someone whose focus is on taking?

A relationship must be win-win—mutually beneficial. But not all of the benefits will be financial. *You* should be concerned with how they get paid and *they* should be concerned with how they can help you. While this may appear idealistic, you should be looking for an advisor who seems unconcerned with how or when he will be compensated. Perhaps that will be because he doesn't need the money (at least not desperately). Perhaps it will be because he just doesn't worry about money. Perhaps it will be because he believes, as he should, that all good work is rewarded.

Discovering what really does motivate a potential advisor can be a very enlightening exercise. Try asking them why they are in this business. Or how long they expect to stay in the business. In their responses look for an interest in the business that transcends the financial rewards. If someone responds, "I get to make a lot of money," watch out. If they say, "I like helping people," that's obviously better.

Ask them about how they get paid and try to determine from their response what motivated them to choose the route they took. Consider if that will allow you to build the kind of relationship you are looking for.

Finally, ask the questions directly. "What motivates you? What gets you up in the morning?" The answers to these questions can be very revealing.

> *"The man who will use his skill and constructive imagination to see how much he can give for a dollar, instead of how little he can give for a dollar, is bound to succeed."*
> Henry Ford

It will most certainly put them on the spot and tell you a lot about how comfortable *they* are sharing their personal values and beliefs with you. Remember, a relationship is a two-way street. Don't let *them* ask all the questions.

As you can see, finding a financial advisor is a lot more like finding a spouse than it is like finding an electrician (no offense to electricians). The ongoing relationship that should develop and endure places a great degree of importance on some of the more emotional issues that we often not only overlook, but actually avoid.

Perhaps you feel the description of the "perfect advisor" created here is too idealistic. Are there really competent financial planners, skilled in a diverse range of financial services, who are motivated to help you and put your best interests first? Absolutely. And more importantly, if more people start looking for this type of advisor, there will soon be a lot more.

> *"If a man is called to be a streetsweeper, he should sweep streets even as Michelangelo painted or Beethoven composed music or Shakespeare wrote poetry. He should sweep streets so well that all the hosts of heaven and earth will pause to say, 'Here lived a great streetsweeper who did his job well.'"*
> MARTIN LUTHER KING JR.

Finding this type of advisor will prove to be immensely rewarding. With a trusted friend, confidant, counselor and money expert working by your side, on your side, and selflessly looking out for your financial well-being, you can truly relax your attention on money and focus on life's more important aspects. And that, dear reader, is just about everything else that life has to offer.

SUMMARY OF KEY POINTS

Finding a financial advisor means finding someone who can help you create a financial plan that will accomplish the six objectives set out in chapter five. To find this person, we should focus on three areas:

1. Relationship. You want a long-term relationship, so focus on finding an advisor you trust and respect—one who is willing to listen, has similar values and beliefs, and is motivated to help.
2. Skills and abilities. You need to look past the designations and find out if the advisor can do, and is doing, the things you want.
3. Motivation. Everyone (even you) is motivated by money. How an advisor gets paid is *not* the issue. The issue is what *really* motivates this advisor—why is she or he in the business?

ACTION STEPS

Start interviewing potential advisors. Take your time. Start with those advisors recommended by other people you trust and respect.

If you already have a good advisor, focus on the relationship. What could you do to make it even better? When was the last time *you* said thanks?

7

LIVING THE LIFE
YOU WERE MEANT TO LIVE

*"The greater danger for most of us is not that our aim is too high
and we miss it, but that it is too low and we reach it."*
MICHELANGELO

THE life you were *meant* to live. By emphasizing the word *meant*, a great many readers will conjure up the notion of fate or determinism. Indeed there are many who *believe* that all is predetermined. Few of those will be (or should be) reading a book on financial planning.

It is not with a fatalistic attitude that I want to talk about the life you were meant to live. It is with an attitude of abundance. It is with an attitude of unlimited happiness. That sounds pretty good, doesn't it?

Here it is.

The life you were meant to live is unbounded. You can quite literally have anything, be anything, and do anything you want. The only limitation is your own imagination.

Read that again. In fact, read it a couple of times. Now take a piece of paper and write down all the reasons why you believe that is *not* true. Now take your pencil and circle all of the reasons that have anything to do with money.

The statement is true. We believe it is otherwise. What we believe frames—limits, if you will— our reality. One of the biggest obstacles in our present reality is our perception of money. More specifically, our perceived lack of money.

> *"Knowledge of what is possible is the beginning of happiness."*
> GEORGE SANTAYANA

I find it disturbing that so many people, and so many financial professionals in particular, see financial planning as a way of "harnessing" your cash flow. I truly question the usefulness of a plan that calls on you to make "sacrifices" to your current lifestyle in order to pay for a future one, or that pushes your dreams into the distant future and pulls them back to earth by limiting their scope to today's resources only. One of the goals of financial planning should be to *eliminate*, or at very least *overcome* obstacles, not make you more aware of them and more limited by them.

Furthermore, any form of financial planning, whether that be retirement planning, estate planning, risk management, whatever, should not only assist you in making a better future, but also a better now! A tall order indeed. But quite achievable. And very powerful.

> *"Life is ours to be spent, not to be saved."*
> D.H. LAWRENCE

Most of the trouble we face when trying to overcome the money obstacle relates to our perception of money or, as some put it, our relationship with money. We tend to see money as either good or evil. We feel deserving or undeserving of it. We are wrapped up emotionally with the thoughts of having or not having money, in some cases to the extent that we can spend very little of our emotions anywhere else.

In truth, money is neither good nor evil. Money does not flow to us based on our "deservedness." Our emotions are ill spent on money, because, after all, it's not really money we want.

Money isn't what life is about. Money is a concept created by man. A matter of convenience to help us in our struggle to cooperate and develop our "interdependence." We continue to struggle with money's ultimate value. As we quickly become a global community we are unsure how to compare currencies of different cultures, and this uncertainty causes wild fluctuations in exchange rates. Is the US dollar the ultimate currency? Perhaps gold? Perhaps neither?

Money, as you can see, is man-made. It is not a force of nature. If we run out of air, or food, or water, we risk death. Not so with money—although some believe it to be so.

Yet one cannot deny that money is an integral and important part of our life in civilized society. It does in fact buy our food, perhaps even our water, and someday maybe our air. In that sense, it *is* a vital life source.

> "Money isn't everything
> —but it's a long way ahead
> of what comes next."
> EDMUND STOCKDALE

More importantly, for today at least, money provides us with many of the comforts and pleasures associated with our lives. Our house, the car we drive, the kind of vacations we take, and the clothes we wear, are all determined, in large part at least, by our access to money. Our society is divided along economic lines. We tend to live in the same neighbourhoods, and associate with those who have similar bank accounts.

So while money may not be important to our happiness, the life we have chosen does depend on money. We could continue on this circular dialogue indefinitely. Let me get to the point.

Let's look at our statement again. The life you were *meant* to live is unbounded. You can, quite literally, have anything, be anything, and do anything you want. The only limitation is your own imagination.

It is most interesting to note that many of us feel our lives *would* be unbounded, if we had unlimited access to money. Most of us believe that money is the ultimate power. Our society promotes that belief by pushing to the top those who acquire or have the most. But even these people will tell you that money isn't what provides happiness.

Remember, the magic ingredient in realizing our dreams is belief. We don't believe our life is unbounded. We do believe that one of those boundaries is money. Those beliefs make both statements true.

> *"May you live all the days of your life."*
> JONATHAN SWIFT

Wait a minute, you may say, money pervades almost every aspect of our lives, and we have a *limited* supply. Isn't that a boundary?

There are two points to make here. First, money is only a tool. Second, the money supply is unlimited. Let's look at each of these.

Money is Only a Tool

It is not money we want, but what money buys that we want. In some instances money buys us material things, like cars, houses and vacations. These we can quantify. These things we can plan to buy and work towards. Other things are not tangible, like security and peace of mind, power and stature. We believe money buys these things as well. They are difficult, if not impossible, to quantify. In our efforts to acquire these things, we generally find it impossible to set goals. There isn't enough to satisfy their purchase, since in truth nothing is being purchased.

Tangible things can be bought with money. The intangibles cannot. To quote The Beatles, "Money can't buy me love." It is useful to be able to make this distinction, and even more useful to live your life in accordance with this understanding.

For the purposes of this book (as this really is a big subject) the essential issue is this. Use money, as much as you need, to satisfy the material needs and wants that accompany your life. Financial planning provides us with the tools to do just that. But accept that your life is more, much more in fact, than what money can buy.

Happiness is *not* linked to money. Happiness is found inside. Money is found outside. It's as simple as that.

Having said all that, it's important to say, and it's essentially the reason for this chapter, that you should have all you want in non-material *and* material things. All you want.

Money is not good or evil. Wanting lots of money because you have lots of reasons to spend the

> "I never admired another man's fortune so much that I became dissatisfied with my own."
> CICERO

money is not wrong. Wanting very little money is also not wrong. Wanting financial security, independence and peace of mind is normal, and healthy. But one must first understand that money is man-made. It's a tool, like a hammer or a pair of scissors. Money in itself has no value and provides no happiness. As a tool, it is perhaps our most important. It provides us with the opportunity to get many of the things and experiences that we want and in some cases need.

Focus then not on money, but on what it is that you really want. Constantly ask yourself that question. What is it you *truly* want? It *isn't* money.

If you are sensing a paradox within this concept that's good. Most of life's greatest truths are wrapped in a paradox.

Let's look at the second point.

The Money Supply is Unlimited

Economists are cringing at the very thought. Philosophers are smirking. You are wondering.

Most of us operate with money as if it were a zero-sum game. I must get money at the expense of someone else. Thus, our business relationships become adversarial. We seek win-lose arrangements. We play unfair, tilting the game to our advantage. We see ourselves as either the conqueror, usually the rich—or the victim, usually the poor.

Intuitively we know this can't be the truth. And it isn't.

At its simplest level, the way to understand this is to see that our money supply is in a state of constant growth. Do you really believe that there is the same amount of "money" in the world today as there was 1000 years ago? Or even 10 years ago? Obviously not. In a very real sense, you create more money when you participate in our economy. When you buy something, build something, or sell something you *create* more value. Our economy truly operates on the basis of win-win relationships. We trade what we don't want—our money—for something we do want. The recipient of the money in turn does the same thing with the money received, and so on. Each time the money changes hands, it is in fact increased or multiplied.

Now let's look at these two new beliefs. Money is only a tool, (it's not money we want, but what money buys that we want), and the supply of money is unlimited. If we could truly operate from these beliefs, what would we likely do?

Most likely we would spend a lot of money. Well, maybe not. Believing that *the* money supply is unlimited is a lot different than believing that *our* money supply is unlimited. So once again, our limitations rest on our beliefs. In this case, the beliefs we hold about who we are, what economic strata we reside within, and what kind of income we can produce vis-a-vis our job.

This discussion is rather circular, isn't it? We would like to believe that we can have, do, and be more, but our present circumstances would indicate that such a belief is foolish. So we wish. We buy lottery tickets. We dream about finding a handsome and rich prince, or the daughter of a millionaire. Our future depends entirely on some external event. But it doesn't.

Perhaps one of the most important and exciting transformations taking place in our world today is the increasing awareness that our external world is shaped by our inner world. That what we believe to be true inside, becomes our truth outside. The greatest journey that lies ahead of mankind is not a journey to distant planets, but rather a journey to the innermost recesses of our thoughts and our mind.

The life you were meant to live is the life you have always imagined. That is why you imagine it. That is what you want. You may have suppressed that life. Your confusion between what is possible and what is just imaginable, between what you want and what others want you to want, between your willingness to be unique and your desire to conform, may have buried that life. But it's still there.

> "Become a possibilitarian.
> No matter how dark things
> seem to be or actually are,
> raise your sights
> and see possibilities
> —always see them,
> for they're always there."
> NORMAN VINCENT PEALE

Your life's mission is to find it, and live it.

Imagine a life in which your needs are met effortlessly, you thoroughly enjoy every aspect of every day—including your work—

and your growth is perpetual. You have everything you want. You love your life and all of the people in it. Your ever-growing understanding of life increases your happiness with each new day. Sure it sounds idealistic, but isn't it exactly what we all want?

Does this life require money? Well, no...and yes. Between us and this life in Shangri-La lies our present-day world—far less than the perfect world we might imagine. Our present-day world does involve money. In fact, for many, money is the focus of the majority of our thoughts. It tops the list of things we worry about. It is the immovable obstacle. No amount of daydreaming or philosophizing is going to get that rock to move.

Enter financial planning. (You were wondering if there was some connection, weren't you?) If you have read the book thus far (and I sure hope you have), then you should readily accept the next few points. First of all, the real power in a financial plan is the fact that it helps us to believe in our goals. Our goals emerge from the financial plan, which is initiated by our vision of our future. Our vision of our future is what we are talking about here and now.

We might not be able to jump across the great chasm between today and the future we imagine. But we can build a bridge. The first and usually most important obstacle we are trying to bridge is money.

Financial planning puts you face to face with what you probably see as your most significant limitation. It forces you to size up your present situation, and assess how your current strategies are likely to cause your future to unfold. Then you can compare what you find with what you want to find. The tension you feel at the very thought is actually a very important component of making your dreams come true. It's excitement. It's believing in the possibilities. It's wondering how they can come true. It's turning on the reception devices that will allow you to see the opportunities that will help you. It's sending a message to the universe of what you want and believe, because the universe *will* give you exactly that.

Change, and moreover growth, is our natural state. We cannot and do not remain stationary. We are constantly looking for ways to do things better, and faster. We want more than our parents had, and we want even more for our children. This has been true for all of time. It's what makes belief in progress so easy. It's the cornerstone of our free-market system.

It is futile, and even unnatural, for us to try to hang on to the status quo. Yet that is exactly what many do. They build their future on "more of the same." They defensively protect their assets, their money, for fear of "falling behind." In a win-lose picture of the world, they believe that hanging on is the only option other than taking at someone else's expense, or being victimized by those who take from them.

In a world of natural growth and abundance for all, a world in which money is only a tool with unlimited supply, we can, and indeed should, set our sights on our true potential. We can have that which we imagine, and money may or may not be an integral part. If it is, it will be there.

> "...you are the eternal possibility, the immeasurable potential of all that was, is and will be."
> DEEPAK CHOPRA

Financial planning allows us to quantify that. Through planning we can take a picture of the present and the future and ask ourselves, *Is this what I want?* Is this where I want to devote my time and energy? Financial planning helps us, by evaluating potential outcomes, to use our tools (one of which is money) and our time, to get the life we really want.

We have all heard someone say, "She is lucky because she always knows what she wants." Indeed, this is a great truth. Knowing *what* you want is far more important than knowing how to get it. What you want is on its way to you. The secret to happiness is not getting what you want, but wanting it after you get it. And knowing what you want next.

This may seem like rather philosophical material to include in a book about financial planning. After all, financial planning to most is a purely left-brain exercise. It's about numbers and logic—tax laws, rates of return, and other non-bendable laws of mathematics. The reason I believe it is important to include this chapter is partly to point out that this assumption is not only untrue, but also quite detrimental to your self-fulfillment.

> "Happiness depends,
> as Nature shows,
> Less on exterior things
> than most suppose."
> WILLIAM COWPER

I also want to point out that this book makes no comment on whether you should have a lot of money or a little money. While I did state that your happiness isn't tied to money, that's not the same as saying you shouldn't have all you want. You should have all you want—or more precisely, all that you *need* in order to have, be and do all that you want.

Finally, the amount of money you can have has no limit. The only limitation is your imagination, and your belief. Make plans that push the limits of those beliefs. As those plans become "realistic," stretch them again. Your beliefs will change. So will your life.

Ultimately, as you gain an increasing understanding of the connection between your inner world and your outer world, between your beliefs and your physical experiences, you will learn to realize your goals in ways that surpass the need to build plans. Today you must set goals, build and follow plans, and realize the fulfillment of the goal. Eventually, the planning phase will shorten and become less important. At some point, perhaps, the planning phase will become unnecessary. You will go from goal setting to goal achieving with effortless ease.

Ironically then, the *ultimate* goal of financial planning is to help you see that a financial plan is unnecessary. This is progress. This is the way of our paradoxical world. Embrace financial planning as a tool to move you forward. But don't hang on so tight that it ultimately holds you back.

SUMMARY OF KEY POINTS

The life you were meant to live is unbounded. You can literally have anything, be anything, and do anything you want. The only limitation is your own imagination.

One of the most significant obstacles we face in trying to accept this statement as truth is money. Financial planning is a powerful tool to help us face and overcome that obstacle.

ACTION STEP

Write down all of the reasons you can't have exactly what you want. Circle those that have anything to do with money. Build these things into your financial plan.

_____

_____

_____

_____

8

THE RULES OF THE GAME

"Thought is the original source of all wealth, all success,
all material gain, all great discoveries and inventions,
and of all achievement."
CLAUDE M. BRISTOL

WHETHER we see it as good or bad, money is a part of our lives from the moment we are born until the moment we die. It is among the most powerful contributors to our sense of personal fulfillment. It is arguably the greatest obstacle en route to reaching our dreams.

And yet, to most, money is largely a mystery. Despite the fact that financial books are perennial best-sellers, and despite the fact that we are attending seminars and training sessions in increasing numbers, and despite the fact that financial services is one of the fastest growing sectors of our workplace, a true understanding of money continues to elude us. Money eludes us. Money is a leading cause of stress. We worry more about money than we do about dying (according to the *Book of Lists*). We study mutual fund tables and reports from experts trying to find the best investment, then choose one, only to change our mind a few days, weeks, or months later. We worry that we are paying too much tax, or if we are paying too little we worry that we may face an audit.

Many have become slaves to money. They work in jobs they don't like—because of the money. They deal with advisors they don't like—because they are making or saving them money. They buy things they believe to be second-rate—because it saves them money. They limit the things they really want to do, like travel, or play a sport or a favourite hobby—because of money. They live only a fraction of the life they really want, because of what? Money.

> *"Within you right now is the power to do things you never dreamed possible. This power becomes available to you just as soon as you can change your beliefs."*
> MAXWELL MALTZ

The main problem is a lack of understanding of what *really* drives our decisions with money. What *do* we believe to be the most important rules of the money game? That's really quite simple. Almost all investment planning is done around three simple premises. Increase return or yield, reduce taxation, and minimize risk. Everything else is a distant second.

Please don't think that I am suggesting that these are unimportant, but they are *not* as important as the rules we overlook. In fact, *they* are the distant second.

Here are the rules of the money game, in no particular order. They are all important. Ignore any of them at your peril.

Listen to Your Emotions

This is exactly the opposite advice you would expect to receive from a left-brain, analytical, financial advisor, isn't it? Don't expect to hear it from a lot of them. But we often ignore our emotions and make decisions based on rational and logical thought, only to make an emotional decision later that costs us plenty.

Take Mary as a classic example. Mary feels that her emotions have kept her "out of the game" and decides that she has been sitting on the side-line, investing in GICs, for too long. So she does some research, gets some advice, and puts $10,000 into a stock, let's call it the ABC Company. Immediately, she's worried. Her emotions tell her that this was a very bad move, but logic is telling her it's the right thing to do. She is determined not to cave in to her emotions, but every day the first thing she looks for in the newspaper is the closing price of ABC Company.

After two weeks her $10,000 has increased to $10,800 and she is ecstatic. She should have done this sooner. She resists the temptation to invest more. Another two weeks later her investment is worth $9,000 and she is seriously depressed. She can't resist the temptation to sell and "get off this rollercoaster ride."

Mary made a rational and logical decision to buy. She convinced herself that she could be a "long-term investor." Despite the nervousness she felt, and she felt plenty, she went ahead and invested. After two weeks her emotions confirmed that she had made a good choice and it was all she could do not to invest more. Then when the stock sank, her emotions screamed at her that this kind of investment was a mistake. She could no longer ignore her emotions. In the end, Mary lost $1,000.

This is the classic example. But it's just one example. Emotions not only significantly impact our money lives, they affect every area of our lives. We ignore them at great risk. Sure you could argue that if Mary had ignored her emotions and kept the stock she would probably have been okay. But that depends on your definition of okay. Mary doesn't want to live in torment today so that she can secure a better rate of return on her money and have more later. Neither should you.

> *"Wealth is the product of man's capacity to think."*
> AYN RAND

There are products, an increasing number of them in fact, that would allow Mary to participate in greater growth opportunities, while also protecting her down-side risk. These products, which some advisors see as "expensive," and for the foolish investor only, are probably what Mary should have been looking for.

We tend to think of money as being a purely left-brain issue. It's about rates of return, taxes, compound interest—lots of mathematical stuff. That's the red herring. Think about it. Here's the ledger.

	Dreams	2
+	Desires	+ 2
+	Beliefs	= 4
-	Fears	
=	Results	

Which side do you suppose holds more power? If you think that money is purely logical, then you will continue to follow the old rules and you will continue to struggle to reconcile your logical decisions against your emotional template. If you agree that money is an emotional subject, then you should start to treat it that way.

A word of caution is warranted. I am not suggesting that you follow your every emotional whim, and end up with a very fast sports car, an oversized house, a fat credit card bill and eventually on medication for self-induced stress. It's important to note that your emotions are like water in an ocean. They are at different depths. Those on the surface are easily influenced and disrupted. They change often, like waves. A small stone can easily make a big splash. But the water that is deep, like the deeper emotions, is not easily changed or affected. Those emotions run true. They are not influenced by the wind and objects on the surface—or by advertising and the greener grass on the neighbour's side of the fence.

Generally speaking, you will recognize the shallow emotions as *reactions*. We react to the news, to the ad on television, and to words spoken to us at a seminar. Reactions are usually short-lived. We come to our senses eventually, and realize that a deeper emotion is more accurate. The deeper emotions may be recognized as our intuition. This is the belief that hangs on despite our desire to react. It's when something resonates as a common-sense, undeniable truth that we know our deeper emotions have been touched.

It's that deeper level of emotion you are trying to tune into. And this deeper level of emotion will teach you the most about yourself, and what you truly want.

One of the things to look for in a good financial advisor is someone who attempts to get in touch with your emotional relationship with money. There are some excellent tools

> "As I grow older, I give far greater respect to my instincts and to the natural reservoir of intuition that slumbers within each one of us."
> ROBIN SHARMA

available for advisors to do that and, of course, nothing beats a sincere interest and a free-form dialogue. Look for advisors that ask questions like, "How does that make you feel?" No, you aren't looking for a psychiatrist who moonlights as a financial advisor, but you are looking for someone who recognizes the importance of emotions in making financial decisions—someone who therefore won't lead you into making what appears to be a rational decision that you will later regret.

We have a great tendency as human beings to believe that all of us should operate from the same set of "logical" criteria. So you can easily find many educated advisors who will try desperately to convince you that your emotions are ill-founded, and more importantly detrimental to financial success. In a nutshell, they are trying to sell you *their* emotions. They may even believe that they can help you to feel differently—more like them. Don't believe them.

Math is a subject of one right answer: 2 + 2 always equals 4. Money is a subject with an infinite array of right answers. What works for you, won't work for someone else. There are hundreds, no thousands, of financial products out there for your consideration. If there were one absolute best way, there would be just one product.

With this understanding of the importance of emotions, and a knowledge of what your emotional relationship with money actually is, you are armed to build an appropriate financial plan. From that financial plan you can find appropriate financial products that will fulfill the objectives of your plan, and take you to the realization of your dreams.

You may need products with more or less risk, more or less guarantees, more or less potential for return. You may need to stretch into areas of discomfort, but you will do that knowing you are doing so, and knowing that your emotions have been given full consideration. When the emotions surface, and tell you that a mistake has been made, you can review all the reasons why you *knew* that would happen and, hopefully, confirm your original decision.

So suppose you are faced with a new and exciting strategy. It is designed to reduce taxes, or increase your returns, or minimize your risk, or it's the deal of all deals, and it's going to do all three. But you just don't quite understand it. How do you decide what to do? Check your feelings. If you don't have a green light there, keep asking questions, or walk away. There's a better way for you to invest. Of that you can be sure.

We deal with money on an emotional level. Accept it. Believe it. Build plans that recognize it.

Money Needs to Circulate, and You Need to Have Fun

Once again, this rule defies logic. If I get money, and never give any of it away, I will continually have more money. How can this *not* work? With this in mind we often build plans that reduce or stifle our spending and focus on sheer accumulation. Eventually, however, we choke off the supply. Our pool of money stagnates, just like the Dead Sea.

Money, as we have discussed, really has no value other than the value we give it. We have given it value for one reason only—so that we can trade it for something we truly *do* want. The minute we use money, it has value. While we hang onto it, its value remains latent, and somewhat uncertain.

More importantly, circulating money helps to multiply it. Every time money changes hands something new of value has entered the economy. Growth in economic terms depends, heavily, on the constant circulation of money. Your personal growth depends on it too.

The absolute best way to circulate money is to *give it away*. Be generous. At one point in my career I was under the guidance of a very well respected manager. He was admired for his business acumen, and feared for his toughness. Without knowing Bob, most would assume that he was not generous because he was so focussed on his own personal "bottom line."

One day Bob took me aside and offered his congratulations on my recent successes. My income was rising rapidly, and of course Bob was benefiting from that. What he said next surprised me. He asked me how much I was giving to charity or my church. I reluctantly told him. He quickly let me know that it wasn't enough. In his words, "You

> *"He who obtains has little. He who scatters has much."*
> LAO-TZU

are giving enough, when it's more than you think you can afford to give."

That was perhaps the best piece of advice he ever gave me—although I still struggle with it.

The rules of money may more appropriately be called the laws of the universe. This one can be restated as *If you want something, give it away.* If you want love, you must give love. If you want respect, you must give respect. If you want trust, you must give trust. If you want money, you must give money.

Business owners will often say that cash flow is king. Cash flow *is* king, both for business and for you. But flow implies flowing in and *out*. Keep money circulating. Use the resulting flow to obtain all the material things your heart desires.

Which leads to another great way to circulate money. Have fun with it. Deepak Chopra says the goal of all other goals is happiness. If you can do something with your money that will bring you happiness, go for it. Make sure you don't focus so much attention on buying a *thing* like a house or a car, that you forget to have fun. You'll end up hating the thing, because it drained away your fun.

When all is said and done you will own absolutely nothing. If anything at all can travel with you into the next life, it will be your memories, and what you learn from your experiences. Make them great.

It's Not a Race

On any day in any newspaper you can find the daily changes in mutual fund prices. In most newspapers you will also find a list of the "biggest movers" for the day. Many people read this, and wonder why their funds never make the Top Ten list. Eventually they switch funds, looking for the faster train.

These people invariably lose at a game where their only competitor is themselves.

Human beings seem to be naturally wired to make all the wrong moves when trying to actively manage investments that move up and down. We are strongly motivated to buy those investments that have most recently been moving up the fastest and farthest, and we can't resist selling those that have moved down. So our instincts cause us to buy too late, and sell at a time which ensures we will lose. We do this largely because we see investing as a race.

When you believe money accumulation is a race, you can't help but look over at the train next to you, and if it's moving faster, jump on. Despite the fact that the train you're on is scheduled to reach the station at the time you planned to arrive, it's human nature to think "but if I got there sooner, it would be better!"

I suppose that's true, to some extent—unless of course no one is there to pick you up and you end up waiting at a deserted train station. But in the investment world, when you see yourself in a race, you actually increase your chances of falling *behind*.

Moreover, it *can't* be a race, because you shouldn't be in a hurry to get *anywhere*. If your life isn't great now you should change it—now. If you are waiting for some magical point in your life when you can stop working and finally enjoy the fruits of your labour, you are in for a major disappointment.

> *"If you cannot work with love but only with distaste, it is better that you should leave your work…"*
> KAHLIL GIBRAN

Life is truly the eternal moment. There is no other time or place than here and now. Work at improving, constantly, that moment. There's no hurry. Here and now will always be here (and now).

Make a plan. Follow the plan. Don't worry about the guy who appears to getting there faster. He's not going where you're going.

The concept of money accumulation being a race is actually a very powerful tool in the arsenal—for financial advisors and money management companies. And they use it. They will try to convince you that since it's a race, what you need is an excellent race-car driver (being them, of course).

You don't need a race-car driver. Accumulating money, like life, is not a race.

Simplify

In case you aren't convinced that money accumulation is a race, the marketing gurus have another ace up their sleeve—you probably will agree that money is complex. So, if you don't need a race-car driver, you probably at least need a mechanic.

Anything in life can become all-consuming. Look around you and you will find those who are consumed by love or lack thereof. You will find those consumed by mind-altering substances. You may even find some who are consumed by cars, by a game, or perhaps by tomatoes. Most certainly you will find many who are consumed by money.

As we give money more and more of our attention, it will become increasingly complex. This is in part due to our increased level of understanding of the many properties we assign to it, and our need to find new and higher stimulation from money itself. It can, and will, quickly become your obsession. You will forget why you want it. You will find yourself playing the many games we have created with money as the prize. Such is the lure and seductiveness of gambling that is spreading like wildfire across North America.

As with anything in life, the key is balance. And in the case of money, in order to put money in its place, one must simplify.

> *"All great things are simple...."*
> WINSTON CHURCHILL

Your objective should be to minimize the time you spend worrying about, or organizing, your financial life. You should free yourself to do what's really important. Money is supposed to let you *do* the important things, not *become* one.

Combine this with the understanding that "it's not a race," and you begin to see the importance of enjoying the trip.

When You Invest, Use Three Guidelines—Your Time Horizon, Your Money Personality, and Your Plan

First of all, let me say that only reluctantly do I include this as a "rule of the game." These three tips are good rules for investing. Investing is another subject entirely.

Nonetheless, the three simple guidelines for investing outlined here are relevant to the overall discussion. So here's a few words to expand on these ideas.

Investing is remarkably simple when you follow this advice, and quite painful and stressful when you don't. For example, don't buy long-term investments (equities) when you have a short time-horizon (if, for example, you need the money next year to buy a house). Don't pay for guarantees when you have no fear of market volatility. Pay for them if you do. And develop an investment plan. Then follow it—ignoring all the news and the bits of advice that will tell you to do something else. You have a plan. All the advice you receive will be from those who don't know your plan, and probably don't have a plan themselves. They are the ones jumping off the train, just before it's most likely to speed up.

Hire an Expert

To continue our train analogy, hire an engineer. Your job isn't to drive the train. Your job is to enjoy the trip.

It's easy to get all caught up in fees, and in fears that you are being "sold." And when you do, you will miss out on one of the best investments you can make. A trusted advisor, with the skills and interest necessary to get you on the right track and keep you there, *can* be found. If you don't have one now, start looking.

You shouldn't pay more taxes than necessary. You should get the most return for the least amount of risk possible, within the parameters of how *you* define risk. And you should be able to adapt to new products, new strategies and new tax laws.

But if *you* are going to do this alone, then you will quickly become consumed by you-know-what.

Good financial advisors actually like this stuff. They get charged up helping others steer through the financial pylons that make up a financial plan. Delegate this stuff to them. Then relax and enjoy the trip.

Money Isn't What You Want. Know What Is

The greatest advice in life is "Know thyself." The most important thing to know about money, is that you don't really want it. You want what it buys.

> *"If money is your hope for independence you will never have it."*
> HENRY FORD

Spend some time figuring that out. It's remarkable how easily and effortlessly money flows to those who know exactly what they want to do with it. And how hard and endless it is for people to accumulate money when they simply want to have "enough" so that they can stop worrying. There is no amount that will stop you from worrying.

Know what you want. Know what you want. Know what you want. Am I repeating myself? Good. Now reread Chapter 1. That's the secret. Know what you want. Turn this knowledge into a vision, a plan and some specific goals. The life you want starts moving ever closer, and becomes ever clearer.

So there you have it. Seven key rules to keep in mind when dealing with money. Read these several times over the days, weeks, and months ahead. Make them your new "paradigm" of dealing with money decisions and situations. See how quickly your world improves as you begin to line up behind these principles.

> *"There are two things to aim at in life: first, to get what you want; and after that to enjoy it. Only the wisest of people achieve the second."*
> LOGAN P. SMITH

Eventually these rules will be your nature. You will not see the world through dollar signs. You will see the world as your playground. Money will simply be another tool in the box.

SUMMARY OF KEY POINTS

We are pretty much convinced that the rules of the money game are: increase yield, reduce taxes, and minimize risk. Everything else is a distant second.

Actually, there are *seven* rules that are considerably more important:

1. Listen to your emotions.
2. Money needs to circulate, and you need to have fun.
3. It's not a race.
4. Simplify.
5. When you invest, use three guidelines—your time horizon, your money personality, and your plan.
6. Hire an expert.
7. Money isn't what you want. Know what is.

ACTION STEPS

Reread these seven rules several times. Eventually your money paradigm will change, and your relationship with money will improve, instead of inhibit, your life.

Write a cheque, right now, to your favourite charity and drop it in the mail.

Set a date with a friend or spouse to go to dinner, or to the theatre, or to do something else you like to do, but haven't done for some time.

9

STARTING NOW

"I hear and I forget. I see and I remember. I do and I understand."
CHINESE PROVERB

KNOWING what to do is definitely the first step. The change you are seeking, however, will only materialize if you actually take action and do it.

As outlined in Chapter 2, the greatest obstacle we face in finding the financial haven we seek is our inability to take the action step required. We don't set an appropriate financial goal—one that gets us emotionally involved and leads us, almost effortlessly, to our desired result.

As you may have discovered in the pages here, and in your own life experiences, this deceptively simple step is remarkably difficult to do. Most of us need a plan, involving a number of steps and probably some outside assistance, just to figure out what we want, how to quantify what we want,

> *"Wisdom is knowing what to do next, skill is knowing how to do it, and virtue is doing it."*
> DAVID STARR JORDAN

and how to pursue what we want. Our world is littered with distractions, with illusory diversions, with signs that appear to point us in the right direction, all the while leading us away from our goal. We need a map. We may need a guide. We need to learn the difference between real and imagined.

Hopefully, some of this is clearer now than before you read this book. But all will not be clear, indeed can never be clear, until you *experience* this for yourself. The map, however good it is, is not the territory. And it's the territory you want.

> *"Last night I asked*
> *an old wise man to tell me all*
> *the secrets of the universe.*
> *He murmured slowly in my ear,*
> *'This cannot be told,*
> *but only learned.'"*
> RUMI

This chapter will present you with a sequential list of things to do—steps, if you will, that will help you take the biggest step of all, stick with it, and in the process change your life. These steps are not the keys to the palace. They are experiences—experiences that will *help you* to find the keys to the palace. Those keys are in you. Only a journey of self-discovery, a journey within, will help you discover them.

Here, then, is the series of action steps that will take you on that journey. Write these steps on a piece of paper, or in your journal, and put a ✓ beside each one when you have completed it.

Enjoy the journey.

Step 1: Make a Commitment to Change

This seems obvious and easy. It hardly seems like an "action" step. So make it one. Right now, wherever you plan to put your list of steps, write the first one, "Make a commitment to change." Now, put a ✓ beside it. You have now taken action. You have made a decision. You have *decided* to change.

Here's what this means. It means that things are going to be different. Lots of things. You will need to do things you have never done before. You will find yourself in situations that make you feel uncomfortable. You will need to try things that put you outside your comfort zone. Every time you feel compelled to "retreat," to go back to the old way of doing things—back to the old you—review the steps you have taken so far. Look at the ✓ beside this step. Recognize that feeling uncomfortable was a conscious choice you made. It's a good thing. You're on the right track.

Without this commitment, without a true resolve to accept the discomfort of a new way of seeing, doing, believing, and being—you are doomed to failure. *Reinforce* this commitment, however, and you forge ahead. And ahead is where you want to be.

> *"Things don't change. You change your way of looking, that's all."*
> CARLOS CASTANEDA

Step 2: Write a Personal Vision Statement

I know what you're saying—"Whoa there! Slow down! I don't know how to write a vision statement!" No problem, I'll tell you how. This truly *is* an action step; unfortunately it's just one that most people are not comfortable with. Failure to follow this step…hey, just reread step number one. See what I mean?

First of all, let's relieve a little of the stress that this step creates. Here are some important facts.

1. No one else ever needs to see, read, or know about this vision statement. It's yours alone. No one will criticize or judge. Throw out your inhibitions. They are limiting and destructive in this exercise. The only opinion that matters here is yours.

2. This step isn't "Write *the* personal vision statement." It's "Write *a* personal vision statement." You will change your vision—often. Don't worry about getting it right the first time. It will never be perfect, in that you will always find ways to improve

it. But you must get started. You can't improve that which doesn't exist. Start somewhere—anywhere.

3. You don't need to have any particular set of skills to do this. Shakespeare's vision statement would be no more powerful than your own will be. You are communicating with yourself and no one else. Speak to yourself in the same way you think to yourself.

Now here's the way to do this. Take a clean sheet of paper (or your computer) and write a few paragraphs describing all of the things you want to be, do, and have. Write in the first person, present tense. This is very important. Writing in future tense keeps it forever locked in the future. Writing it in present tense makes it real, today. For example, you might write something like "I am a loving father and have a wonderful relationship with my children." Or, "I am a successful business woman, respected by my peers." Or, "I have a beautiful home in the country with five bedrooms, a wonderfully landscaped property with a pool, and no mortgage."

> *"You can't do anything about the length of your life, but you can do something about its width and depth."*
> SHIRA TEHRANI

Of course you may write all the above, and more. Consider all aspects of your life: your family and friends, your career, your spirituality, your community, your character. Everything important should be covered.

In Covey's *Seven Habits of Highly Effective People* he clearly highlights the importance of the vision statement to all aspects of your life. And he offers some excellent suggestions with respect to how to get this started. Among those suggestions is the idea of writing your own eulogy. Imagine yourself at your own funeral, many years from now, of course. If you could be the architect of your life (and you can) and you became all that you truly desire to be (and you will) what would people say about you as they said goodbye? Imagine the speeches delivered by your spouse, boss or co-worker, spiritual leader, member of your community, and any other important figure in your life. Now take their words, and turn them into your own.

Get something down in writing. Read it often. Change it often. Feel the magnetic power of what your heart desires, once you *know* what that is.

Remember, the indispensable first step in getting the material things you want in life—or the money to buy those things—is this: *know what you want.* Then decide to get it.

Your vision of the future contains the seeds of everything you want, and everything you will have, be and do. The exercise of writing, reading, and revising your personal vision statement connects the inner world with the outer world. It moves you deeper on your inward journey, all the while sending clear signals to the physical world to guide you on your outer journey—your journey through life.

Write a personal vision statement. And put a ✓ beside this on your list of steps.

Step 3: Organize Your Financial Life

The number one vision-killer is money, or, more accurately, a perceived shortage of money. To overcome this, you need to develop a different attitude towards money—a new paradigm. And you will need a plan.

The first step to making a change in your relationship with money is to get organized. If you are already an organized person with respect to money, congratulations. Move on to the next step. If not, do the following.

Create an itemized list of all of your assets and liabilities—basically, a balance sheet. Get all of the investment statements or reports that pertain to these assets and liabilities and put them into one file or folder.

Next, review your chequebooks, credit card statements, etc., and construct a budget of monthly and annual expenses. Don't worry, this isn't something that you should see as eventually becoming a tool to make you spend less (avoid advisors who attempt to do this). It is merely a way of getting organized, and getting to know more about yourself. You may decide on your own to change your spending habits when you review your budget against your vision, but only you can decide this. (You may have already done a budget and balance sheet while reading Chapter 4—if not, there is a sample balance sheet and budget form in Appendix I.)

Chances are, after you complete this step, you are going to feel a lot different. A lot better.

Step 4: Find a Financial Advisor or Decide, Firmly, Not To

Many religions describe hell as the "world between worlds," a place where you remain in permanent limbo. There are countless people who live in the financial equivalent—the people who constantly struggle with the issue of whether or not they want to involve someone else in their financial lives.

Concern about paying fees, inability to trust, fear of being sold, and the embarrassment of revealing current financial status, are emotional reasons to go it alone. But they lead you into financial purgatory. When these are the excuses, your underlying emotions are telling you that you do want help. But emotions on the surface, usually without any basis, convince you that you shouldn't get help. This conflict causes paralysis.

There is one good reason *not* to get help. That is, you simply enjoy looking after your financial affairs, and the skills you lack (if any) you are seeking to obtain. A growing number of people are taking the necessary courses, and staying abreast of the changing financial landscape because they enjoy it, and they have growing abilities. Some of these people will become financial advisors themselves. The others are do-it-yourselfers.

For the rest, this is an important step. Read carefully the advice in Chapter 6. You aren't trying to find the smartest guy on the street, or the one who made the most money for your friend. You are trying to find a competent advisor with the skills needed to handle your particular issues (issues that will be more apparent to you now that you have a vision statement to guide you). Most importantly, you are looking for an advisor with whom you can forge a lasting, mutually beneficial relationship. A trusted friend, confidant, and coach. Relationships are based on emotional issues. Approach this task this way, and the task itself will be easier.

One of my favourite places is the Metro Toronto Zoo. My two youngest daughters and I are frequent visitors. Recently we went on a special excursion that involved a guided tour of some key areas. Through the guide we learned more than we could have imagined, and we saw things that we had never noticed on our many prior visits. It was as if we were visiting the zoo for the first time.

Find a financial advisor, and the rest of your financial life will be a *guided* trip.

Step 5: Quantify Your Vision—Create a Financial Plan

Give this list to your advisor. Share with him or her the essence of your personal vision, particularly the areas in which money is going to play an important role. Ask for an estimate.

This, of course, is *the* step. It is the one thing that must be done in order to move forward financially. You are building a financial plan, and in the process you will arrive at the all-important goal or goals.

> *"If you have built castles in the air, your work need not be lost; that is where they should be. Now put the foundations under them."*
> HENRY DAVID THOREAU

Set your sights on the financial target that will give you the money you need to realize your dreams. Write this goal, and think of it often. The universe will conspire to help you once you know what it is you want. But the universe needs specifics. How much, and when. This is really all you need to do. Really.

Step 6: Follow Your Plan

Your plan will give you a goal, or goals, and tell you what you need to do to achieve them. So *do* the things you have agreed to do. And do them *now*.

> *"If you want something you've never had, you have to do something you've never done."*
> LIN TEAGLE

If your plan says you will invest $500 per month starting now, then start now. Postpone this until whatever it is you need to get past happens, and you have just jumped off the train. To return, you will need to go back to step number one and go through the entire process again.

If you have issues that require you to postpone saving money, for example, these should have been dealt with in the plan. Your plan, in this case, may actually call for you to do nothing for the next few months or years.

Work on the plan until it makes sense and until you can commit to the action steps called for. DO NOT accept a plan that asks you to do something you don't intend to do.

That being the case, you have a plan, you made a commitment to it, it was designed to get you exactly what you want. *So do it.*

The changes you seek are well underway.

Step 7: Let Go

If you have done all of the previous six steps (some of which are ongoing) then the only thing left to do is to let go. Stop worrying and fretting. Don't check the paper every day to see if your investments are on track. Don't make an appointment with another advisor to see if they have any ideas that are better than your current advisor's ideas. Don't compare your plan to that of a neighbour or co-worker.

Let go. What you have set out to make happen is going to happen. The only thing that can stop your plans from being realized at this stage is you. The only thing that will derail you is a lack of faith, or a diminishing commitment.

All the powers of the universe are now at work making your vision a

> *"An integral being knows without going, sees without looking, and accepts without doing."*
> LAO TZU

reality. Don't get in the way. Watch for and follow the signs. You will know the signs by the fact that they point to a higher way— to more—to a bigger vision than you previously dared to imagine. The signs that point to failure, to confusion, or to worry are an illusion. You created those signs yourself. Ignore them.

Letting go is the most difficult step of all, but I am sure that it is also far and away the most powerful. It's also the step we most often trip over. We obsess over things, and this obsession leads to worry and worry becomes perpetual. We need to stop thinking about what we *want*, and let go, accepting it as already ours. When we do, we will have it.

> *"The moment I let go of it was the moment I got more than I could handle."*
> ALANIS MORRISETTE

I will confess, that while many of the steps and ideas I have outlined remain a challenge for me to understand and adhere to, letting go is without question the most difficult. There is an essence to this issue that is difficult to comprehend, and even more difficult to articulate. In many ways it's the ultimate paradox. We need to focus our time and energy on determining what we want, and then in order to get it, we need to lose our attachment to it.

Yes, *letting go* is not easy. And yes, it sounds reckless and careless. Just remember the great spiritual principle we should all follow: "Don't be stupid." Be courageous, be daring, take risks, but trust your intuition, your deepest emotions.

So when an opportunity—a new job, or change in career, for example—presents itself as you pursue your new vision, ask yourself, "If this worked, would it take me closer to my vision?"

> *"These, then, are my last words to you: Be not afraid of life. Believe that life is worth living and your belief will help create the fact."*
> WILLIAM JAMES

When the answer is yes, you are witnessing the universe at work—at work for you. You've been given a sign. A door has been opened for you. Follow the sign, and walk through the door. Let go of the old way. A new way has been created.

Still, there's more. An even better vision lies in waiting. There are things you can do, have, and be that you can't yet imagine. But you will. For now, enjoy the journey.

SUMMARY OF KEY POINTS
AND
ACTION STEPS

Accomplishing anything requires action. These are the action steps you need to take to move towards the future you want, and the future you have yet to imagine.

1. Make a commitment to change.
2. Write a personal vision statement.
3. Organize your financial life.
4. Find a financial advisor or decide, firmly, not to.
5. Quantify your vision—Create a financial plan.
6. Follow your plan.
7. Let go.

SOME THOUGHTS IN
RETROSPECT

WHEN I started writing this book—almost two years ago—I believed (arrogantly perhaps) that my views on financial planning were unique. But as I talked with advisors about what I wanted to say, and about how I believed a financial services organization needed to serve, I realized that my views are far from unique. In fact, few people with whom I have spoken disagree to any significant degree at all.

What remains true is that financial services organizations—life insurance companies, banks, stock brokerages, financial planners—all find themselves in a struggle between the old paradigm of doing business, which has worked for decades, and the new paradigm, which on the surface contradicts much of what they believe to be true. Most financial services organizations have been built around a transactional model. More transactions equals more money. Selling and sales form the basis of determining success or failure. Relationships are important, but only as a means to more sales. In short, things are still being done according to an old, outdated set of beliefs.

What needs to change, and in fact *is* changing, is the underlying assumption. All businesses, and most certainly financial services, need to be measured by the quality of their relationships.

This is particularly appropriate in financial services, given the assumption that what financial advisors need to do, first and foremost, is to assist clients in making sense of money in the business of living their lives. They need to help them find the power to obtain money, and use money, as a servant to fulfill all aspects of their personal visions. How can financial advisors do that if they, too, are slaves to money? A fellow inmate of the prison cannot free you. Those on the other side of the bars *can*.

If this transformation ever completely takes place, it won't be without a great deal of pain, discomfort, and uncertainty. Money will no longer hold the mysterious power it now possesses. This book won't be necessary. Financial advisors won't be necessary.

Therein lies the paradoxical struggle for financial advisors in trying to do the right thing. Just as cancer researchers wrestle with the idea that their ultimate success (finding a cure) will cost them their jobs, so too must financial advisors operate within the framework of trying to do their job so well, that they become unnecessary to their clients.

In an unbounded view of our lives, that doesn't matter. There is a better way to do literally everything we now do, including everything done by financial planners. We can only begin to move towards an understanding of a better way, when we let go of the old way.

We have been clinging to our deep-rooted beliefs about money for a long time. Some of the ideas put forth in this book may have left you doubting. I hope so. I wasn't trying to write a book to improve on the old way. I want to explore a new way. And it is indeed an exploration. If you have thoughts or ideas that might help us move further on this journey, we'd very much like to hear from you. Send us a note, or an e-mail.

And thanks for reading my book.

Bill Bell
Aurora, Ontario
December 1999

APPENDIX I

SAMPLE BUDGET FORM

THE categories listed provide a general guideline of the most common expenses. Feel free to regroup to suit your personal circumstances and add categories as needed.

Date: _____

EXPENSE ITEM	CURRENT ANNUAL AMOUNT	EXPECTED AMOUNT IN RETIREMENT (TODAY'S DOLLARS)
Mortgage (monthly payments)		
Property taxes		
Heat, hydro, water		
Home insurance		
Cable/TV		
Life insurance		
Car:		
• monthly payments		
• gas, maintenance		
• insurance, licence		
• parking		
Public transportation		
Other loan payments		
Clothing		

continued on page 148

Sample Budget Form
(continued)

EXPENSE ITEM	CURRENT ANNUAL AMOUNT	EXPECTED AMOUNT IN RETIREMENT (TODAY'S DOLLARS)
Personal/hair/cleaners		
Childcare, babysitting		
Pet care		
Groceries		
Other household		
Gifts (birthday/seasonal)		
Furniture & decorating		
Dining out/entertainment		
Sports & recreation		
Education savings (RESP)		
Healthcare		
RRSP & savings		
Travel and vacation		
Other		
Other		
Other		
Other		
TOTALS		

APPENDIX II

SAMPLE BALANCE SHEET
OR NET WORTH STATEMENT

Date: _____

	SELF	SPOUSE	COMBINED
ASSETS			
Cash & chequing accounts			
Savings account			
Other cash			
Non-registered investments			
Stocks & bonds			
GICs			
Other investments			
Real estate (not residence)			
Registered investments			
RRSP			
Money purchase pension			
Locked-in plans			
Personal assets			
Residence			
Personal valuables			
Cottage			
Vehicles			
Other			
TOTAL ASSETS (A)			

continued on page 150

Sample Balance Sheet or Net Worth Statement
(continued)

	SELF	SPOUSE	COMBINED
LIABILITIES			
Mortgage on home			
Consumer loan			
Investment loan			
Credit card			
Other debt			
TOTAL LIABILITIES (B)			
NET WORTH			
Total assets (A)			
Total liabilities (B)			
NET WORTH (A - B)			

SUGGESTED READING

THIS book may very well leave you with some unanswered questions. That's perfectly all right. Information on the ideas and principles outlined here can be found in countless books. In order to assist you in selecting which book(s) you should read next, I decided to include this "Suggested Reading" section. I have further decided that I should keep this list short—a kind of "deserted on an island" list of *only* the most influential and inspiring books on specific related topics.

So here, in no particular order, are my top 12 recommendations of books you should own and read to further your quest for money, and life, mastery.

The Seven Habits of Highly Effective People, by Stephen R. Covey (Fireside, 1989). Okay, they are in no particular order except this one. If I had to recommend just one book, this would be it. In many respects this is the modern guidebook to being human.

The Monk Who Sold His Ferrari, by Robin Sharma (Harper Collins, 1997). This powerful and elegant narrative will start you on a journey to happiness. When you've finished this one, read the rest of Robin Sharma's growing library.

The Millionaire Next Door, by Thomas J. Stanley and William D. Danko (Longstreet Press, 1996). Quite often the reason new ideas are hard to embrace is because old beliefs are taking up the space. Read this book and forever dispel some of the misconceptions you probably hold about who is rich and how they got that way. Not a light read, but in many respects an eye-opener.

Simple Living In A Complex World, by David Irvine (RedStone, 1997). The title says it all. David Irvine's simple message is simply told and will no doubt cause you to challenge some of your present paradigms in search of the balance we all crave.

Inspirational Leadership, by Lance Secretan (Macmillan, 1999). Yes, this is a book about leadership, which may lead you to believe that only CEOs should read it. That would be too bad. The message of hope and inspiration in this book is one that we should all hear.

The Seven Spiritual Laws of Success, by Deepak Chopra (New World Library, 1994). Deepak Chopra has written many wonderful books, but this is perhaps the most all-encompassing from the master of blending science with spirit.

Winning the Tax Game 2000, by Tim Cestnick (Prentice Hall, 1999). Okay, this might not be a book you actually sit down 152152and read, although it is arguably the only tax guide that you could. For those seeking a technical guide and reference book, Tim has cornered the market.

Quantum Leap Thinking, by James J. Mapes (Dove Books, 1996). The subtitle, "An Owner's Guide to the Mind," sums it up. If you are wrestling with how to implement change, especially a change in beliefs, this is your book.

The Energy of Money, by Maria Nemeth (Ballantine, 1997).
Whether we admit it or not, we have a relationship with
money which has a profound effect on how much we have
and keep. This book is a great way to explore this issue
more deeply with some terrific exercises to assist you on
your journey of self-discovery.

Psycho-Cybernetics, by Maxwell Maltz (Prentice-Hall, 1960).
If you are having trouble accepting the importance of goals
and beliefs, read this book.

Think and Grow Rich, by Napoleon Hill (Ballantine, 1960).
The timeless classic, perhaps still ahead of its time, and most
certainly well ahead of its time when written.

The Roaring 2000's, by Harry S. Dent, Jr. (Simon Schuster, 1998).
If you are going to read books that predict doom and gloom,
at least read this book for balance. Harry Dent's outlook is
marvelously optimistic, and he has a track record of getting
it right.

How to Contact Us

To learn more about Bell Financial Inc.
their services, products and publications

please contact us at

15165 Yonge Street, Suite 201
Aurora, Ontario L4G IMI

Telephone: (905) 713•3765
Fax: (905) 713•2937
e-mail: mail@bellfinancial.on.ca
website: www.bellfinancial.on.ca
toll free: 1 (888) 367•7450

Volume discounts are available for this book.

One Step to Wealth
*...you're **that** close to the life you want*